DATE DUE

JUN 0 6			
AUG 5 09			
GAYLORD			PRINTED IN U.S.A.

D1023399

in association with

magazine

Wedding Bouquets

Over 300 designs for every bride

JACKSON COUNTY LIBRARY SERVICES
MEDFORD, OREGON 97501

First published in Great Britain in 2006 by
Hamlyn, a division of Octopus Publishing Group Ltd
2–4 Heron Quays, London E14 4JP

Copyright © Octopus Publishing Group Ltd 2006

All rights reserved. No part of this work may
be reproduced or utilized in any form or by any
means, electronic or mechanical, including
photocopying, recording or by any information
storage and retrieval system, without the prior
written permission of the publisher.

ISBN 0 600 61386 0
EAN 9780600613862

A CIP catalogue record for this book is available
from the British Library

Printed and bound in China

10 9 8 7 6 5 4 3 2 1

Contents

Introduction

Once you've chosen the perfect outfit for your big day, choosing your flowers is the most enjoyable – but possibly the most difficult – of all the decisions that lie ahead. With so many bouquet styles and colour choices it's easy to feel overwhelmed, but the range of flowers featured here will help you to find the perfect bouquet for your wedding. Each chapter follows a colour theme, from paler to darker shades, and offers a range of floral styles to choose from. If you are looking for something a little different, the final chapter (see page 296) provides ideas for more unusual bouquets.

Choosing a Florist

Most brides find that hiring a professional florist is the best way to ensure that the flowers they carry, and all of the additional wedding flowers, are arranged beautifully and last the day without wilting. However, if you have chosen an intimate ceremony, you may feel confident that you and your friends can organize the flowers that will be needed. If this is the case, be sure to practise with flowers of the same variety a few weeks in advance, to check that the arrangements will still look good by the end of the celebrations. Also check that the flowers you want to use in your bouquet and other arrangements will be available at the time of your wedding and within your budget (see page 12). You will be responsible for ordering all the flowers and foliage needed well in advance so make sure that you have a reliable supplier.

Word of mouth is often the best way to find a florist. If a friend or even a friend of a friend has recently been married, they will usually be pleased to talk about the ceremony and to pass on the name of the person who was responsible for their flowers. They should also have plenty of photographs of the arrangements for you to look at before you contact the florist. Failing a word-of-mouth recommendation, your local classified telephone directory or the internet will provide you with some possible names to follow up. If the reception is at an hotel or other venue where weddings are regularly celebrated, ask for their advice: they might even have an arrangement with a local florist.

Before you make a final decision, make sure that you see photographs of other weddings and large-scale events that the florist has worked on and, if at all possible, speak to some of the people involved in previous events. An experienced florist should be able to suggest flowers that will suit your dress style and the venue, as well as your budget, but it also helps if you have an idea of the type of flowers and style of bouquet you would prefer, and here it is worth spending time looking at magazines, books or other people's wedding photographs. Your florist should also want to find out about you and your character, and about how the flowers you will be choosing will reflect your personality and bring your dreams to life. These face-to-face meetings are essential, and if the florist you have approached does not suggest such meetings, think again and look at the next name on your list.

Make your plans well in advance – at least six months ahead is usual – so that there are no clashes and so that all the flowers and foliage, as well as any of the other decorative elements that might be needed, can be ordered in time. Your florist should make time to accompany you on visits to the church (if appropriate) and the place where the wedding reception will be held. Something as simple as the colour of the carpet and soft furnishings in a hotel's dining room needs to be taken into account in the overall colour scheme. You also need to consider factors such as access to the venue(s), when the flowers should be delivered and who will be responsible for them.

If a close friend or relative presses you to let them help, it might be less stressful for everyone concerned if you encourage them to be responsible for a single display at the reception. Make sure they use the same type of flowers and colours as all the other arrangements, and let your florist know that someone else is involved, albeit on a small scale, so that there are no personality clashes or arguments about who is doing what, where and with which flowers.

Types of Bouquet
Although there are hundreds of flowers to choose from, there are, basically, only a few types of bouquet, and your choice will be largely determined by the style of dress

you have chosen, which, in turn, will have been influenced by your body shape.

The main types of dress include ballerina style, which is ideal for a traditional wedding and which has a full skirt and a fitted bodice. Princess-style or A-line dresses have a flared skirt with vertical seams from the shoulders or waist providing a neat, elegant appearance. The high-waisted skirts of empire-line dresses fall straight from a fitted bust. If you are tall and willowy, you could choose a column, which is straight all the way down, or a tightly fitting mermaid-style dress, which flares out below the hips.

If you are petite, don't choose a large bouquet that will be out of proportion to your shape and size. A small, formal bouquet or a neat tear-drop arrangement will better complement your figure. This type of arrangement will also be appropriate if you are aiming for a more traditional look.

If you are tall and slim and have chosen a bias cut dress, choose a bouquet that will enhance the lines of your silhouette. Shower and trailing bouquets, with long wired stems, graceful sprays of foliage and simple lines, will complement your dress and help you achieve an elegant look. Hand-tied bouquets are also suitable for slim, fitted dresses, but a hand-tied posy can be equally appropriate with a full-skirted dress.

Coordinating the Flowers

Your bouquet is the single most important element to select. Choose the flowers and any ribbons and other decorations first, making sure that the colours and textures of the flowers and foliage are appropriate for the fabric and style of your dress. Then it is time to think about flowers for your bridesmaids, as well as any buttonholes and corsages that have to be made. Find out what your mum and your fiancé's mum will be wearing so that those colours can be coordinated with the flowers. Choose a colour that will blend with the colours in your bouquet or select a single colour that will carried through in all the floral arrangements.

Choosing the Flowers

Today flowers are flown in from all around the world, and it is possible to have popular flowers, such as roses, orchids and tulips all year round. However, you may find that seasonality still affects the cost, so it is best to seek the advice of a florist.

Unfortunately, many of the flowers supplied to florists are not especially fragrant. This is particularly true of roses, which are now often bred for the uniformity of their colour and shape and the length of their thorn-free stems, characteristics that make life easy for flower arrangers and the cut-flower trade but that can be disappointing if you have set your heart on walking down the aisle in a cloud of fragrance. Some modern roses are deliciously scented, however, so make your wishes clear from the outset so that the right variety can be ordered for you.

Some flowers can be relied on to provide sweet scents. Freesias, available in a rainbow of shades, are usually sweetly scented, and the arching stems and funnel-shaped flowers can be used in a variety of bouquet shapes and styles. Many lilies are scented, including the white Madonna lily (*Lilium candidum*) and Easter lily (*L. longiflorum*), and many of the modern hybrids, in colours ranging from the palest pink, though yellow to deep oranges

and reds, are also fragrant. In spring a posy of dainty lily-of-the-valley (*Convallaria majalis*) is hard to beat for its fresh, sweet scent. Jasmine, beautifully scented, is great in trailing bouquets, and fragrant sweet peas (*Lathyrus odoratus*) can be used to add a strong scent to summer posies. Carnations are readily available all year round and with their warm, spicy fragrance work well in autumnal bouquets.

If your wedding is scheduled for late spring or summer, there is another aspect of the flower selection to consider: pollen allergies. Even if neither you nor the groom suffers from hayfever, find out if the bridesmaids and close family members are likely to be affected. Nothing is likely to spoil the occasion more than a bridesmaid continually blowing her nose or your future mother-in-law wiping her eyes, and not because she is shedding tears of joy. Grasses of all types are often used in bouquets for their graceful, arching habit, but the seedheads, which can look great in photographs, will be a particular problem for anyone who suffers from hayfever, as will some types of lily, which have pollen-laden blooms.

How Much Will it Cost?

Traditionally, the cost of the wedding flowers is shared between the bride's and groom's families, with the bride's side paying for the flowers for the wedding reception and the groom's paying for the bouquets carried by the bride and bridesmaids and any other flowers that might be needed to decorate the ceremony location. To avoid any difficulties arising later, put this on your list of things to discuss and decide before you commit yourself to any expenditure.

A professional florist will agree a schedule and budget with you, and you should confirm this in writing. Keep in touch with the florist throughout the planning process, and ensure they are informed of any changes to outfits, location and so on.

If you are organizing the flowers yourself, be realistic about your budget. Magazines will be a useful guide here, and it will be worth spending time looking through as many as you can find to work out how much your dream is going to cost. Some leading florists have their own websites, and these will give you an opportunity to compare prices. If the amount you want to spend on the flowers is limited, look in florists' shops to give you a rough idea of what your favourite blooms are going to cost and don't be afraid to ask for an estimate. By all means draw up your wish list, but be prepared to temper your dreams to reality. Bear in mind too that in high summer your choice will be greater – and usually less costly – than it will be in late autumn or winter.

It's your day. Enjoy it – and whether you throw your flowers for one of your guests to catch or preserve them as a memento, make sure they are the perfect bouquet for you.

White, Ivory and Cream

Bouquet of Calla Lilies and Aspidistra

Flowers calla lilies; aspidistra leaves **Meaning** calla lily: beauty **Scent** none
Construction stems bound with ribbon **Dress** column, mermaid

Bouquet of Orchids and Roses

Flowers phalaenopsis orchids; roses; galax and aspidistra leaves
Meaning orchid: beauty, love, refinement; rose (white):
innocence, purity; galax: encouragement **Scent** slight fragrance
Construction wired stems bound into a handle **Dress** column, mermaid

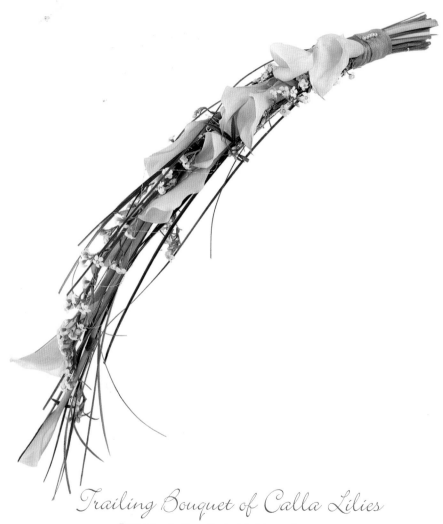

Trailing Bouquet of Calla Lilies

Flowers calla lilies; *Euphorbia fulgens*; bear grass
Meaning calla lily: beauty; euphorbia: persistence; grass: submission **Scent** none
Construction wired stems bound with silver wire and ribbon; decorated with pearl beads
Dress A-line, column, mermaid

Bouquet of Lilies and Roses

Flowers roses; lilies; phlox; snowberries; eucalyptus and aspidistra leaves
Meaning rose (white): innocence, purity; lily: purity of heart; phlox: unity **Scent** strong
Construction hand-tied; wired roses decorated with pearl beads **Dress** A-line, ballerina

Trailing Bouquet of Gypsophila and Orchids

Flowers phalaenopsis orchids; gypsophila; skeletonized magnolia leaves
Meaning orchid: beauty, love, refinement; gypsophila: innocence, purity of heart **Scent** none
Construction wired stems bound with silver wire **Dress** A-line, column, empire-line

Trailing Bouquet of Orchids and Grass

Flowers phalaenopsis orchids; steel grass; ruscus leaves
Meaning orchid: beauty, love, refinement; grass: submission **Scent** none
Construction wired stems bound into a handle **Dress** A-line, column, empire-line

Trailing Bouquet of Stephanotis and Jasmine

Flowers stephanotis; jasmine; gypsophila **Meaning** stephanotis: happiness in marriage; jasmine: amiability; gypsophila: innocence, purity of heart **Scent** very fragrant
Construction wired stems bound into a sisal framework with feathers
Dress ballerina, empire-line

Bouquet of Narcissi and Muscaris

Flowers paperwhite narcissi; muscaris; hebe and cyclamen leaves
Meaning narcissus: regard; cyclamen: modesty **Scent** strongly fragrant
Construction hand-tied **Dress** ballerina, empire-line

Bouquet of Orchids and Chrysanthemums

Flowers phalaenopsis orchids; chrysanthemums; lisianthus; gypsophila; hydrangeas
Meaning orchid: beauty, love, refinement; chrysanthemum: truth; gypsophila: innocence, purity of heart; hydrangea: thank you for understanding **Scent** none
Construction wired stems bound into a handle **Dress** A-line, ballerina

Bouquet of Tulips and Gypsophila

Flowers tulips; gypsophila **Meaning** tulip: love, passion; gypsophila: innocence, purity of heart
Scent none **Construction** wired stems surrounded by silk tulle
Dress A-line, ballerina, empire-line

Hand-tied Bouquet of Freesias

Flowers freesias; stephanotis; muehlenbeckia; skimmia leaves
Meaning freesia: friendship, innocence, trust; stephanotis: happiness in marriage
Scent very fragrant **Construction** hand-tied **Dress** column

Bouquet of Roses and Lysimachia

Flowers roses; lysimachia; hydrangeas
Meaning rose (cream): innocence, purity; hydrangea: thank you for understanding
Scent slight fragrance **Construction** hand-tied **Dress** ballerina, empire-line

Bouquet of Roses and Gypsophila

Flowers roses; gypsophila; aspidistra leaves; equisetum
Meaning rose (white): innocence, purity; gypsophila: innocence, purity of heart
Scent slight fragrance **Construction** wired stems bound into a handle; roses decorated with pearl beads; decorated with silver wire **Dress** column, mermaid

Bouquet of Calla Lilies and Hippeastrums

Flowers calla lilies; hippeastrums; bear grass; hellebore leaves
Meaning calla lily: beauty; hippeastrum: expectation, splendid beauty; grass: submission
Scent none **Construction** wired stems bound into a handle
Dress column, empire-line, mermaid

Sheaf of Eucharis and Lilac

Flowers eucharis; lilac; ruscus leaves
Meaning eucharis: maidenly charm; lilac: modesty, youthful innocence **Scent** strongly fragrant
Construction hand-tied and fastened with ribbon **Dress** A-line, column, empire-line

Trailing Bouquet of Orchids and Roses

Flowers dendrobium orchids; roses; gypsophila; bupleurum
Meaning orchid: beauty, love, refinement; rose (white): innocence, purity; gypsophila:
innocence, purity of heart **Scent** slight fragrance **Construction** wired stems bound into
a handle; decorated with silver wire **Dress** A-line, column, mermaid

Sheaf of Calla Lilies and Roses

Flowers calla lilies; roses; ranunculus; amaranthus; pittosporum leaves
Meaning calla lily: beauty; rose (white): innocence, purity; ranunculus: charm,
radiance; amaranthus: immortality, unfading love **Scent** slight fragrance
Construction hand-tied with raffia **Dress** A-line, column, empire-line

Bouquet of Lily-of-the-valley and Orchids

Flowers lily-of-the-valley; phalaenopsis orchids
Meaning lily-of-the-valley: return of happiness; orchid: beauty, love, refinement
Scent strong, sweet fragrance **Construction** wired stems bound with satin ribbon;
decorated with feathers **Dress** A-line, column, empire-line

Bouquet of Roses and Ornithogalum

Flowers roses; *Ornithogalum arabicum*; steel grass; pittosporum leaves
Meaning rose (white): innocence, purity; grass: submission **Scent** slight fragrance
Construction wire twisted into a handle and a nest; decorated with pearl beads
Dress column, mermaid

Trailing Bouquet of Eucharis and Orchids

Flowers eucharis; cymbidium orchids; chincherinchees; asparagus fern; rose leaves; ivy
Meaning eucharis: maidenly charm; orchid: beauty, love, refinement; asparagus fern: fascination
Scent strongly fragrant **Construction** wired stems bound into a handle
Dress column, mermaid

Bouquet of Hydrangeas and Hypericum

Flowers hydrangeas; hypericum berries and leaves
Meaning hydrangea: thank you for understanding **Scent** none
Construction hand-tied **Dress** ballerina, empire-line

Bouquet of Stephanotis and Orchids

Flowers stephanotis; dendrobium orchids
Meaning stephanotis: happiness in marriage; orchid: beauty, love, refinement
Scent strongly fragrant **Construction** wired stems bound into a handle **Dress** A-line, ballerina

Trailing Bouquet of Tulips and Jasmine

Flowers tulips; jasmine; ivy; jasmine leaves
Meaning tulip: love, passion; jasmine: amiability; ivy: fidelity, wedded love **Scent** none
Construction hand-tied into a frame of weeping willow **Dress** A-line, empire-line

Bouquet of Orchids, Brunia and Aspidistra

Flowers phalaenopsis orchids; *Brunia albiflora*; variegated grass; date palm; aspidistra leaves
Meaning orchid: beauty, love, refinement; grass: submission **Scent** none
Construction hand-tied **Dress** A-line, column

Trailing Bouquet of Roses and Veronica

Flowers roses; veronica; *Alchemilla mollis*; *Brunia albiflora*; bear grass; hosta and ivy leaves
Meaning rose (white): innocence, purity; veronica: fidelity; grass: submission; ivy: fidelity,
wedded love **Scent** slight fragrance **Construction** hand-tied **Dress** column, mermaid

Trailing Bouquet of Eucharis and Calla Lilies

Flowers eucharis; calla lilies; roses; freesias; lisianthus; gypsophila; pepper berries; setaria seedheads; variegated grass **Meaning** eucharis: maidenly charm; calla lily: beauty; rose (cream): innocence, purity; freesia: friendship, innocence, trust; grass: submission **Scent** strong fragrance **Construction** wired stems bound into a handle **Dress** A-line, mermaid

Bouquet of Calla Lilies and Feathers

Flowers calla lilies; ivy; aspidistra leaves
Meaning calla lily: beauty; ivy: fidelity, wedded love **Scent** none
Construction wired stems bound with feathers into a carrying ring
Dress A-line, ballerina, empire-line

Bouquet of Lily-of-the-valley

Flowers lily-of-the-valley and leaves
Meaning lily-of-the-valley: return of happiness
Scent strong, sweet fragrance Construction hand-tied
Dress ballerina, empire-line

Freestyle Bouquet of Calla Lilies

Flowers calla lilies; steel grass; monstera leaf **Meaning** calla lily: beauty; grass: submission
Scent none **Construction** hand-tied **Dress** column, mermaid

Bouquet of Roses

Flowers roses, hosta leaves **Meaning** rose (white): innocence, purity **Scent** slight fragrance
Construction wired stems bound into a handle **Dress** ballerina, empire-line

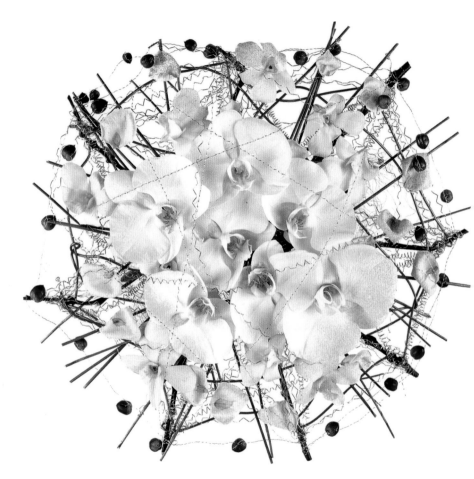

Bouquet of Orchids and Berries

Flowers phalaenopsis and dendrobium orchids; rose petals; hypericum berries; steel grass
Meaning orchid: beauty, love, refinement; rose (white): innocence, purity; grass: submission
Scent slight fragrance **Construction** wired stems bound into a handle;
decorated with bronze wire **Dress** ballerina, empire-line

Shower Bouquet of Eucharis and Roses

Flowers eucharis; roses; hosta leaves; asparagus fern

Meaning eucharis: maidenly charm; rose (cream): innocence, purity; asparagus fern: fascination

Scent strong fragrance **Construction** wired stems bound into a handle

Dress A-line, column, empire-line

Informal Bouquet of Calla Lilies

Flowers calla lilies **Meaning** calla lily: beauty **Scent** none
Construction hand-tied; decorated with red jewels
Dress A-line, ballerina, empire-line

Bouquet of Roses and Galax

Flowers roses; galax leaves **Meaning** rose (cream): innocence, purity; galax: encouragement
Scent slight fragrance **Construction** hand-tied; decorated with silver wire and blue beads
Dress ballerina, empire-line

Bouquet of Roses and Hellebores

Flowers roses; hellebores **Meaning** rose (cream): innocence, purity **Scent** slight fragrance
Construction hand-tied **Dress** A-line, empire-line

Stem Posy of Roses and Freesias

Flowers roses; freesias; calla lilies; bamboo; eucalyptus leaves
Meaning rose (cream): innocence, purity; freesia: friendship, innocence, trust **Scent** fragrant
Construction hand-tied and bound with ribbon **Dress** A-line, column

Bouquet of Ranunculus and Berries

Flowers ranunculus; hypericum berries; birch twigs and catkins; fatsia and rose leaves
Meaning ranunculus: charm, radiance; birch: elegance, grace, meekness
Scent none **Construction** wired stems twisted into a handle and tied with sisal
Dress column, mermaid

Cornucopia of Orchids and Nerines

Flowers dendrobium orchids; nerines **Meaning** orchid: beauty, love, refinement
Scent none **Construction** wired stems bound with gold wire; decorated with pearl beads
Dress ballerina, empire-line

Trailing Bouquet of Roses and Ruscus

Flowers roses; lisianthus; freesias; *Euphorbia fulgens*; asparagus fern; bear grass; ruscus leaves **Meaning** rose (cream): innocence, purity; freesia: friendship, innocence, trust; euphorbia: persistence; asparagus fern: fascination; grass: submission **Scent** slight fragrance **Construction** wired stems bound into a handle **Dress** A-line, column

Trailing Bouquet of Roses and Grass

Flowers roses; guelder rose; bear grass; ivy
Meaning rose (cream): innocence, purity; grass: submission; ivy: fidelity, wedded love
Scent slight fragrance **Construction** wired stems bound into a handle; decorated with silver wire
Dress A-line, ballerina, empire-line

Bouquet of Stephanotis and Ranunculus

Flowers stephanotis; ranunculus; freesias; calla lilies; eucalyptus and galax leaves
Meaning stephanotis: happiness in marriage; ranunculus: charm, radiance; freesia: friendship, innocence, trust; calla lily: beauty; galax: encouragement **Scent** strongly fragrant
Construction wired stems bound into a handle **Dress** ballerina, empire-line

Trailing Bouquet of Roses and Feathers

Flowers roses; stephanotis; lysimachia; scabious seedheads; ivy leaves and berries; ruscus leaves; birch catkins **Meaning** stephanotis: happiness in marriage; rose (cream): innocence, purity; ivy: fidelity, wedded love; birch: elegance, grace **Scent** fragrant **Construction** wired stems bound into a handle; decorated with feathers **Dress** A-line, column, mermaid

Bouquet of Alstroemerias and Freesias

Flowers alstroemerias; freesias; wax flowers; antirrhinums; *Ornithogalum arabicum*; asparagus fern; fatsia and daylily leaves **Meaning** alstroemeria: fortune, prosperity; freesia: friendship, innocence, trust; antirrhinum: strength; asparagus fern: fascination

Scent strongly fragrant **Construction** hand-tied **Dress** column, empire-line

Bouquet of Roses and Ornithogalums

Flowers roses; *Ornithogalum narbonense* **Meaning** rose (white): innocence, purity
Scent slight fragrance **Construction** hand-tied **Dress** ballerina, empire-line

Shower Bouquet of Roses and Calla Lilies

Flowers roses; calla lilies; wax flowers; asparagus fern; bear grass
Meaning rose (white): innocence, purity; calla lily: beauty; asparagus
fern: fascination; grass: submission **Scent** slight fragrance
Construction wired stems bound onto a frame **Dress** column, mermaid

Bouquet of Stephanotis and Ranunculus

Flowers stephanotis; ranunculus; roses; brachyglottis leaves; genista seedheads
Meaning stephanotis: happiness in marriage; ranunculus: charm,
radiance; rose (white): innocence, purity **Scent** fragrant
Construction wired stems bound into a handle **Dress** A-line, empire-line

Trailing Bouquet of Stephanotis and Roses

Flowers stephanotis; roses; ivy leaves and berries; ruscus leaves
Meaning stephanotis: happiness in marriage; rose (white):
innocence, purity; ivy: fidelity, wedded love **Scent** fragrant
Construction hand-tied; decorated with brown wire **Dress** column, empire-line

Bouquet of Carnations and Willow

Flowers carnations; stephanotis; galax and daylily leaves; willow stems
Meaning carnation: devoted love, fascination; stephanotis: happiness in marriage; galax: encouragement **Scent** warm, spicy fragrance **Construction** hand-tied; stephanotis and willow wired with pearl beads **Dress** ballerina, empire-line

Trailing Bouquet of Roses and Clematis Stems

Flowers roses; calla lilies; clematis stems; asparagus fern
Meaning rose (white): innocence, purity; calla lily: beauty; clematis: ingenuity; asparagus
fern: fascination **Scent** slight fragrance **Construction** wired stems bound into a handle;
decorated with glass beads **Dress** A-line, column, mermaid

Bouquet of Lisianthus and Roses

Flowers lisianthus; roses; eucalyptus leaves; skeletonized leaves
Meaning rose (white): innocence, purity **Scent** slight fragrance
Construction hand-tied **Dress** ballerina

Bouquet of Calla Lilies and Hosta

Flowers calla lilies; hosta leaves **Meaning** calla lily: beauty
Scent none **Construction** hand-tied **Dress** A-line, ballerina, empire-line

Bouquet of Roses and Physalis

Flowers roses; physalis and scabious seedheads; ivy leaves and berries; crab apples; ornamental squash **Meaning** rose (cream): innocence, purity; ivy: fidelity, wedded love
Scent slight fragrance **Construction** hand-tied **Dress** A-line, column

Bouquet of Roses and Bear Grass

Flowers roses; bear grass **Meaning** rose (cream): innocence, purity; grass: submission
Scent slight fragrance **Construction** hand-tied; decorated with wired crystal beads
Dress ballerina, empire-line

Crescent Bouquet of Orchids and Roses

Flowers dendrobium orchids; lilies; roses; bear grass; palm and dracaena leaves
Meaning orchid: beauty, love, refinement; lily: purity of heart; rose (white): innocence, purity;
grass: submission; palm: success, victory **Scent** slight fragrance **Construction** wired stems
bound with ribbon; grass decorated with crystal beads **Dress** A-line, column, mermaid

Trailing Bouquet of Roses and Guelder Rose

Flowers roses; guelder rose; hydrangeas; ivy; snowberries
Meaning rose (white): innocence, purity; hydrangea: thank you for understanding; ivy: fidelity,
wedded love **Scent** slight fragrance **Construction** wired stems bound into a handle;
decorated with silver wire and crystal beads **Dress** A-line, column, mermaid

Bouquet of Dahlias and Gerberas

Flowers dahlias; gerberas; roses; bronzed ruscus and salal leaves
Meaning dahlia: dignity, elegance; gerbera: innocence; rose (white): innocence, purity
Scent none **Construction** wired stems bound into a handle **Dress** ballerina, empire-line

Bouquet of Lily-of-the-valley and Gypsophila

Flowers lily-of-the-valley; gypsophila; freesias; lisianthus; hydrangeas
Meaning lily-of-the-valley: return of happiness; gypsophila: innocence, purity of heart; freesia: friendship, innocence, trust **Scent** sweet fragrance
Construction hand-tied decorated with feathers **Dress** A-line, ballerina, empire-line

Bouquet of Roses and Carnations

Flowers roses; carnations; phalaenopsis orchids; hypericum berries; bear grass; grevillea
Meaning rose (cream): innocence, purity; carnation: devoted love, fascination; orchid:
beauty, love, refinement; grass: submission **Scent** warm, spicy fragrance
Construction hand-tied **Dress** ballerina, empire-line

Bouquet of Tulips

Flowers parrot and single tulips; hosta leaves **Meaning** tulip: love, passion **Scent** none
Construction hand-tied **Dress** ballerina, empire-line

Shower Bouquet of Freesias and Roses

Flowers freesias; roses; bear grass; ivy
Meaning freesia: friendship, innocence, trust; rose (cream): innocence, purity; grass:
submission; ivy: fidelity, wedded love **Scent** sweet fragrance **Construction** wired stems
bound into a handle; decorated with feathers **Dress** A-line, column, empire-line

Shower Bouquet of Calla Lilies and Roses

Flowers calla lilies; roses; equisetum; fatsia leaves
Meaning calla lily: beauty; rose (cream): innocence, purity **Scent** none
Construction hand-tied **Dress** column, mermaid

Bouquet of Roses and Ivy

Flowers roses; lisianthus; ivy leaves and berries
Meaning rose (white): innocence, purity; ivy: fidelity, wedded love **Scent** slight fragrance
Construction hand-tied **Dress** ballerina, empire-line

Bouquet of Roses and Chrysanthemums

Flowers roses; chrysanthemums; *Ornithogalum arabicum*; bear grass; phormium leaves; pine shoots **Meaning** rose (cream): innocence, purity; chrysanthemum: truth; grass: submission; pine: hope **Scent** slight fragrance **Construction** hand-tied **Dress** ballerina, empire-line

Bouquet of Roses and Jasmine

Flowers roses; jasmine; camellia leaves
Meaning rose (white): innocence, purity; jasmine: amiability
Scent fragrant **Construction** hand-tied **Dress** ballerina, empire-line

Bouquet of Bouvardia and Carnations

Flowers bouvardia; carnations; roses; galax leaves
Meaning bouvardia: enthusiasm; carnation: devoted love, fascination; rose (cream):
innocence, purity; galax: encouragement **Scent** warm, spicy fragrance
Construction hand-tied **Dress** ballerina, empire-line

Bouquet of Roses and Astrantias

Flowers roses; astrantias **Meaning** rose (cream): innocence, purity
Scent slight fragrance **Construction** hand-tied **Dress** ballerina, empire-line

Bouquet of Gypsophila

Flowers gypsophila **Meaning** gypsophila: innocence, purity of heart **Scent** slight fragrance
Construction hand-tied; decorated with crystal beads **Dress** A-line, column

Bouquet of Roses and Narcissi

Flowers roses; narcissi; pussy willow
Meaning rose (white): innocence, purity; narcissus: regard; pussy willow: motherhood
Scent slight fragrance **Construction** hand-tied **Dress** ballerina, empire-line

Bouquet of Anemones and Ivy

Flowers anemones; lisianthus; lilac; ivy; pussy willow
Meaning anemone: expectation; lilac: modesty, youthful innocence; ivy: fidelity,
wedded love; pussy willow: motherhood **Scent** sweet fragrance
Construction hand-tied **Dress** ballerina, empire-line

Bouquet of Jewelled Roses

Flowers roses **Meaning** rose (cream): innocence, purity **Scent** slight fragrance
Construction hand-tied; decorated with wired jewellery **Dress** ballerina, empire-line

Bouquet of Tulips and Ranunculus

Flowers tulips; ranunculus; hellebores; wax flowers; roses; pieris; guelder rose; narcissi; Queen Anne's lace; pittosporum leaves **Meaning** tulip: love, passion; rose (white): innocence, purity **Scent** slight fragrance **Construction** hand-tied **Dress** A-line, ballerina

Bouquet of Calla Lilies and Guelder Rose

Flowers calla lilies; guelder rose; roses; hypericum berries; bear grass; dracaena leaves
Meaning calla lily: beauty; rose (white): innocence, purity; grass: submission
Scent slight fragrance **Construction** wired stems bound into a handle; decorated
with crystal beads **Dress** column, empire-line, mermaid

Sheaf Bouquet of Orchids and Pussy Willow

Flowers cymbidium orchids; guelder rose; lisianthus; pussy willow; aspidistra leaves
Meaning orchid: beauty, love, refinement; pussy willow: motherhood
Scent none **Construction** hand-tied **Dress** column, empire-line

Bouquet of Orchids and Anthuriums

Flowers cymbidium orchids; anthurium leaves; poppy seedheads
Meaning orchid: beauty, love, refinement **Scent** slight fragrance
Construction hand-tied **Dress** ballerina, empire-line

Bouquet of Lisianthus and Chrysanthemums

Flowers lisianthus; chrysanthemums; roses; dendrobium orchids; chincherinchees; *Hydrangea paniculata*; variegated grass **Meaning** chrysanthemum: truth; rose (white): innocence; orchid: beauty, love, refinement; hydrangea: thank you for understanding; grass: submission **Scent** none **Construction** hand-tied; plaited grass decorated with glass beads **Dress** ballerina

Bouquet of Anthuriums and Amaranthus

Flowers anthuriums; amaranthus; philodendron leaves
Meaning amaranthus: immortality, unfading love **Scent** none
Construction hand-tied; decorated with wire and crystal beads
Dress A-line, column, mermaid

Bouquet of Anthuriums and Carnations

Flowers anthuriums; carnations; ranunculus; moluccella; guelder rose; cymbidium orchids; tulips; lily-of-the-valley; bear grass; bassia, fatsia and aspidistra leaves; palm fronds **Meaning** carnation: love; ranunculus: charm; moluccella: good luck; orchid: beauty; grass: submission **Scent** spicy fragrance **Construction** hand-tied; decorated with glass beads **Dress** A-line

Bouquet of Bouvardia and Roses

Flowers bouvardia; roses; ruscus leaves **Meaning** bouvardia: enthusiasm; rose (green): friendship, joy **Scent** fragrant **Construction** hand-tied **Dress** ballerina, empire-line

Yellow

Bouquet of Roses and Narcissi

Flowers roses; narcissi; rosemary; *Cordyline compacta* leaves
Meaning rose (white): innocence, purity; narcissus: regard; rosemary: remembrance
Scent slight fragrance **Construction** hand-tied **Dress** ballerina, empire-line

Bouquet of Roses and Galax

Flowers roses; galax leaves **Meaning** rose (yellow): friendship, joy; galax: encouragement
Scent slight fragrance **Construction** wired stems bound into a handle
Dress ballerina, empire-line

Bouquet of Ranunculus and Skimmia

Flowers ranunculus; skimmia; roses; viburnum berries
Meaning ranunculus: charm, radiance; rose (red): happiness **Scent** slight fragrance
Construction hand-tied **Dress** ballerina, empire-line

Bouquet of Roses and Rosemary

Flowers roses; rosemary; guelder rose; nerines; phlox
Meaning rose (yellow): friendship, joy; rosemary: remembrance; phlox: unity
Scent fragrant **Construction** hand-tied **Dress** A-line, ballerina, empire-line

Bouquet of Orchids

Flowers cymbidium orchids **Meaning** orchid: beauty, love, refinement **Scent** none
Construction wired stems bound into a handle **Dress** ballerina, empire-line

Bouquet of Orchids and Asparagus Fern

Flowers cymbidium orchids; roses; anthurium; asparagus fern; ruscus leaves
Meaning orchid: beauty, love, refinement; rose (cream): innocence, purity; asparagus
fern: fascination **Scent** slight fragrance **Construction** wired stems bound into a handle
Dress A-line, column, mermaid

Bouquet of Calla Lilies and Leucospermum

Flowers calla lilies; leucospermum; bear grass; fatsia leaves
Meaning calla lily: beauty; grass: submission **Scent** none
Construction wired stems bound into a handle **Dress** A-line, column, mermaid

Formal Bouquet of Roses and Calla Lilies

Flowers roses; calla lilies; galax leaves
Meaning rose (yellow): friendship, joy; calla lily: beauty; galax: encouragement
Scent slight fragrance **Construction** hand-tied **Dress** ballerina, empire-line

Bouquet of Roses and Camellias

Flowers roses; camellias; guelder rose; viburnum berries
Meaning rose (white): innocence, purity; rose (yellow): friendship, joy; camellia: adoration,
perfection **Scent** slight fragrance **Construction** hand-tied **Dress** ballerina, empire-line

Shower Bouquet of Lilies and Orchids

Flowers lilies; dendrobium orchids; astilbes; calla lilies; asparagus fern; bear grass; eucalyptus and hosta leaves **Meaning** lily: gratitude; orchid: beauty, love, refinement; calla lily: beauty; asparagus fern: fascination; grass: submission **Scent** none **Construction** wired stems bound into a handle **Dress** column, mermaid

Bouquet of Chrysanthemums and Orchids

Flowers chrysanthemums; dendrobium orchids; gypsophila; hypericum berries; bear grass; skeletonized leaves; cinnamon sticks **Meaning** chrysanthemum: truth; orchid: beauty, love; gypsophila: purity of heart; grass: submission **Scent** warm, spicy fragrance **Construction** wired stems bound into a handle; decorated with silver wire **Dress** ballerina, empire-line

Freestyle Bouquet of Orchids and Ornithogalums

Flowers paphiopedilum orchids; *Ornithogalum arabicum*; bear grass; fatsia and dracaena
leaves **Meaning** orchid: beauty, love, refinement; grass: submission
Scent none **Construction** hand-tied **Dress** A-line, column, mermaid

Bouquet of Orchids and Green Roses

Flowers cymbidium orchids; roses; hellebores; steel grass
Meaning orchid: beauty, love, refinement; rose (green): friendship, joy; grass: submission
Scent none **Construction** hand-tied **Dress** ballerina, empire-line

Bouquet of Orchids and Aspidistras

Flowers cymbidium orchids; acacia; bear grass; aspidistra leaves
Meaning orchid: beauty, love, refinement; grass: submission **Scent** none
Construction wired stems bound into a handle **Dress** A-line, column, mermaid

Bouquet of Calla Lilies and Ornithogalum

Flowers calla lilies; *Ornithogalum arabicum*; roses; snowberries; crocosmia seedheads;
philodendron leaves **Meaning** calla lily: beauty; rose (yellow): friendship, joy
Scent none **Construction** hand-tied **Dress** ballerina, empire-line

Bouquet of Orchids and Ruscus

Flowers cymbidium orchids; roses; ruscus leaves
Meaning orchid: beauty, love refinement; rose (yellow): friendship, joy
Scent slight fragrance **Construction** hand-tied **Dress** A-line, column, empire-line

Formal Bouquet of Roses

Flowers roses **Meaning** rose (cream): innocence, purity; rose (yellow):
friendship, joy; rose (orange): desire, enthusiasm, fascination **Scent** fragrant
Construction hand-tied **Dress** ballerina, empire-line

Bouquet of Gerberas and Marguerites

Flowers gerberas; marguerites; roses; camomile; daylily leaves; love grass
Meaning gerbera: innocence; rose (white): innocence, purity; grass: submission
Scent none **Construction** hand-tied with raffia **Dress** ballerina, empire-line

Bouquet of Roses and Guelder Rose

Flowers roses; guelder rose; eucalyptus and ophiopogon leaves **Meaning** rose (yellow): friendship, joy **Scent** slight fragrance **Construction** hand-tied **Dress** ballerina, empire-line

Bouquet of Narcissi and Forsythia

Flowers narcissi; forsythia; tulips; hard ruscus; dried clematis vine; solidago; tree fern
Meaning narcissus: regard; forsythia: anticipation; tulip: love, passion **Scent** none
Construction hand-tied **Dress** ballerina, empire-line

Hand-tied Bouquet of Calla Lilies

Flowers calla lilies; asparagus fern **Meaning** calla lily: beauty; asparagus fern: fascination
Scent none **Construction** hand-tied; bound with ribbon and decorated with copper wire
Dress A-line, column, mermaid

Bouquet of Tulips

Flowers tulips Meaning tulip: love, passion Scent none
Construction hand-tied Dress ballerina, empire-line

Bouquet of Sunflowers and Berries

Flowers sunflowers; eucalyptus leaves; milfoil; hypericum berries; *Brunia albiflora*
Meaning sunflower: devotion, loyalty, pride **Scent** none
Construction hand-tied **Dress** ballerina, empire-line

Bouquet of Roses and Jasmine

Flowers roses; jasmine **Meaning** rose (yellow): friendship, joy; jasmine: amiability
Scent fragrant **Construction** hand-tied; encased in a framework of trailing jasmine stems
Dress ballerina, empire-line

Bouquet of Sunflowers and Grasses

Flowers sunflowers; love grass; wheat; fatsia leaves
Meaning sunflower: devotion, loyalty, pride; grass: submission; wheat: prosperity
Scent none **Construction** hand-tied with raffia **Dress** ballerina, empire-line

Bouquet of Roses and Monstera Leaves

Flowers roses; steel grass; eucalyptus and monstera leaves
Meaning rose (yellow): friendship, joy; grass: submission **Scent** slight fragrance
Construction hand-tied; decorated with pearl beads threaded on to twisted golden wire
Dress ballerina, empire-line

Bouquet of Sunflowers

Flowers sunflowers; bronzed and skeletonized leaves
Meaning sunflower: devotion, loyalty, pride **Scent** none
Construction hand-tied **Dress** ballerina, empire-line

Bouquet of Calla Lilies and Wax Flowers

Flowers calla lilies; wax flowers; phalaenopsis orchids; poppy seedheads; love grass; ophiopogon leaves **Meaning** calla lily: beauty; grass: submission
Scent none **Construction** hand-tied **Dress** ballerina, empire-line

Peach and Orange

Bouquet of Roses and Tea Tree

Flowers roses; rosemary; tea tree
Meaning rose (peach): desire, enthusiasm; rose (white and cream):
innocence, purity; rosemary: remembrance **Scent** sweet fragrance
Construction hand-tied **Dress** ballerina, empire-line

Bouquet of Roses and Heather

Flowers roses; tree heather; senecio and brachyglottis leaves
Meaning rose (peach): desire, enthusiasm; heather: protection **Scent** strong, sweet fragrance
Construction hand-tied **Dress** ballerina, empire-line

Bouquet of Anthuriums and Aspidistra Leaves

Flowers anthuriums; *Brunia albiflora*; cucumis fruit; bear grass; daylily and aspidistra leaves
Meaning grass: submission **Scent** none **Construction** wired stems bound into a handle
Dress A-line, mermaid, column

Bouquet of Orchids and Moluccella

Flowers paphiopedilum orchids; moluccella; roses; hellebores; ivy; fatsia leaves
Meaning orchid: beauty, love, refinement; moluccella: good luck; rose (green):
joy, friendship; ivy: fidelity, wedded love **Scent** slight fragrance
Construction hand-tied **Dress** ballerina, empire-line

Tear-drop Bouquet of Lilies

Flowers lilies; craspedia; kangaroo paw; dubium; leucadendrons; kalanchoe;
dracaena and dieffenbachia leaves **Meaning** lily: purity of heart **Scent** fragrant
Construction wired stems bound into a handle **Dress** A-line, column

Bouquet of Anthuriums and Carnations

Flowers anthuriums; carnations; hypericum berries; ivy
Meaning carnation: devoted love, fascination; ivy: fidelity, wedded love
Scent warm, spicy fragrance **Construction** hand-tied **Dress** ballerina, empire-line

Bouquet of Tulips and Palm Fronds

Flowers tulips; palm leaves **Meaning** tulip: love, passion; palm: success, victory **Scent** none
Construction hand-tied **Dress** ballerina, empire-line

Sheaf Bouquet of Calla Lilies

Flowers calla lilies; dendrobium orchids; hypericum berries; fountain and steel grasses; aspidistra leaf **Meaning** calla lily: beauty; orchid: beauty, love, refinement; grass: submission
Scent none **Construction** hand-tied; decorated with gold wire and beads
Dress A-line, column

Informal Bouquet of Calla Lilies and Orchids

Flowers calla lilies; arachnis orchids; rose hips; daylily leaves
Meaning calla lily: beauty; orchid: beauty, love, refinement **Scent** strong fragrance
Construction hand-tied **Dress** A-line, column

Sheaf Bouquet of Gerberas and Physalis

Flowers gerberas; physalis seedheads; roses; lilies; crocosmia buds; ruscus leaves; palm fronds
Meaning gerbera: innocence; rose (orange): desire, enthusiasm, fascination; rose (red):
happiness; lily: purity of heart; palm: success, victory **Scent** strong fragrance
Construction hand-tied with raffia **Dress** A-line, column

Formal Bouquet of Roses

Flowers roses; nerteras **Meaning** rose (yellow): friendship, joy; rose (orange): desire, enthusiasm, fascination; rose (red): happiness **Scent** strong fragrance
Construction wired stems bound into a handle **Dress** ballerina, empire-line

Sheaf Bouquet of Tulips and Pussy Willow

Flowers tulips; pussy willow; rudbeckia
Meaning tulip: love, passion; rudbeckia: justice; pussy willow: motherhood **Scent** none
Construction hand-tied with ribbon; decorated with bronze wire **Dress** A-line, column

Bouquet of Ranunculus and Anemones

Flowers ranunculus; anemones; ivy; daylily leaves
Meaning ranunculus: charm, radiance; anemone: expectation; ivy: fidelity, wedded love
Scent none **Construction** hand-tied **Dress** ballerina, empire-line

Shower Bouquet of Calla Lilies and Proteas

Flowers calla lilies; proteas; globe thistles; asparagus fern; aspidistra leaves
Meaning calla lily: beauty; asparagus fern: fascination **Scent** none
Construction wired stems bound into a handle; decorated with silk butterflies and silver wire
Dress A-line, column, mermaid

Bouquet of Calla Lilies and Hydrangeas

Flowers calla lilies; hydrangeas; roses; viburnum berries; ivy
Meaning calla lily: beauty; hydrangea: thank you for understanding; rose (orange):
desire, enthusiasm, fascination; ivy: fidelity, wedded love **Scent** slight fragrance
Construction hand-tied **Dress** ballerina, empire-line

Bouquet of Anthuriums and Fritillaries

Flowers anthuriums; fritillaries; umbrella and asparagus ferns; hypericum berries; galax leaves
Meaning fern: sincerity; asparagus fern: fascination; galax: encouragement
Scent none **Construction** hand-tied; decorated with copper wire **Dress** ballerina, empire-line

Bouquet of Calla Lilies and Croton Leaves

Flowers calla lilies; gerberas; roses; bear grass; croton and aspidistra leaves
Meaning calla lily: beauty; gerbera: innocence; rose (orange): desire,
enthusiasm, fascination; grass: submission **Scent** slight fragrance
Construction hand-tied; decorated with crystal beads **Dress** column, empire-line

Formal Bouquet of Roses and Sunflowers

Flowers roses; sunflowers; calla lilies; celosias; hebe and salal leaves; ornamental pineapples
Meaning rose (orange): desire, enthusiasm, fascination; rose (red): happiness;
sunflower: devotion, loyalty, pride; calla lily: beauty **Scent** strong fragrance
Construction wired stems bound into a handle **Dress** ballerina, empire-line

Sheaf Bouquet of Calla Lilies and Rudbeckias

Flowers calla lilies; rudbeckias; oncidium orchids; beech leaves
Meaning calla lily: beauty; rudbeckia: justice; orchid: beauty, love, refinement; beech: prosperity
Scent none **Construction** hand-tied **Dress** ballerina, empire-line

Bouquet of Celosias and Calla Lilies

Flowers celosias; calla lilies; roses; hypericum and ivy berries; lotus seedheads
Meaning calla lily: beauty; rose (red): happiness; ivy: fidelity, wedded love
Scent strong fragrance **Construction** hand-tied **Dress** ballerina, empire-line

Bouquet of Anthuriums and Proteas

Flowers anthuriums; proteas; calla lilies; rudbeckias; typha; hebe and dracaena leaves
Meaning calla lily: beauty; rudbeckia: justice **Scent** none
Construction hand-tied; decorated with red wire
Dress ballerina, empire-line

Bouquet of Hellebores

Flowers hellebores; silver birch **Meaning** birch: elegance, grace, meekness **Scent** none
Construction wired stems bound with ribbon **Dress** column, mermaid

Red

Bouquet of Gloriosas and Orchids

Flowers gloriosas; cymbidium orchids; celosias; asparagus fern
Meaning gloriosa: glorious beauty; orchid: beauty, love, refinement; asparagus fern: fascination
Scent none **Construction** wired stems bound into a handle **Dress** A-line, column, mermaid

Bouquet of Freesias

Flowers freesias **Meaning** freesia: friendship, innocence, trust **Scent** strongly fragrant
Construction hand-tied with ribbon and decorated with a buckle **Dress** ballerina

Bouquet of Roses and Rosemary

Flowers roses; rosemary **Meaning** rose (red): happiness; rosemary: remembrance
Scent fragrant **Construction** hand-tied with ribbon **Dress** ballerina, empire-line

Bouquet of Holly and Roses

Flowers roses; calla lilies; guelder rose; ivy; holly, pittosporum, phormium and hebe leaves; pine cones **Meaning** rose (red): happiness; calla lily: beauty; ivy: fidelity, wedded love; pine: hope **Scent** strong fragrance **Construction** wired stems bound into a handle; rose petals decorated with silver wire **Dress** ballerina, empire-line

Bouquet of Gerberas and Leucadendrons

Flowers gerberas; leucadendrons; miniature hippeastrums; hypericum berries; salal leaves
Meaning gerbera: innocence; hippeastrum: expectation, splendid beauty
Scent none **Construction** wired stems bound into a handle **Dress** ballerina, empire-line

Bouquet of Roses and Lachenalia

Flowers roses; lachenalia; hypericum berries **Meaning** rose (red): happiness
Scent strong fragrance **Construction** hand-tied **Dress** ballerina, empire-line

Trailing Bouquet of Roses and Gerberas

Flowers roses; gerberas; tulips; asparagus fern; skeletonized leaves
Meaning rose (red): happiness; tulip: love, passion; gerbera: innocence; asparagus
fern: fascination **Scent** strong fragrance **Construction** wired stems bound into a handle;
decorated with wired rose petals and feathers **Dress** A-line, column

Bouquet of Hippeastrums

Flowers hippeastrums; bear grass
Meaning hippeastrum: expectation, splendid beauty; grass: submission **Scent** none
Construction wired stems tightly bound with ribbon; decorated with glass beads
Dress ballerina, empire-line

Bouquet of Amaranthus and Hippeastrums

Flowers amaranthus; hippeastrums; anthuriums; roses; leucadendrons; phormium leaves
Meaning amaranthus: immortality, unfading love; hippeastrum: expectation,
splendid beauty; rose (red): happiness **Scent** slight fragrance
Construction wired stems bound into a handle **Dress** A-line, column, mermaid

Bouquet of Roses and Gloriosas

Flowers roses; gloriosas **Meaning** rose (red): happiness; gloriosa: glorious beauty
Scent strong fragrance **Construction** hand-tied with ribbon **Dress** ballerina, empire-line

Bouquet of Gerberas and Anthuriums

Flowers germini gerberas; anthuriums; roses; hypericum berries; galax and holly leaves; pine needles **Meaning** gerbera: innocence; rose (red): happiness; galax: encouragement; pine: hope **Scent** slight fragrance **Construction** wired stems bound into a handle; pine needles wired to create cascade **Dress** A-line, column, mermaid

Spray Bouquet of Calla Lilies

Flowers calla lilies **Meaning** calla lily: beauty **Scent** none
Construction wired stems bound into a handle; decorated with ribbon, silver wire and beads
Dress A-line, column, mermaid

Bouquet of Roses

Flowers roses; camellia leaves **Meaning** rose (red): happiness; camellia: admiration, perfection
Scent strong fragrance **Construction** hand-tied **Dress** ballerina, empire-line

Bouquet of Roses and Ivy

Flowers roses; ivy; willow **Meaning** rose (red): happiness; ivy: fidelity, wedded love
Scent strong fragrance **Construction** hand-tied; willow framework **Dress** ballerina, empire-line

Bouquet of Roses and Berries

Flowers roses; hypericum berries; milfoil **Meaning** rose (red): happiness
Scent strong fragrance **Construction** wired stems bound into a handle; decorated
with gold wire and wired rose petals **Dress** ballerina, empire-line

Cone Bouquet of Calla Lilies and Orchids

Flowers calla lilies; dendrobium orchids; beech leaves
Meaning calla lily: beauty; orchid: beauty, love, refinement; beech: prosperity **Scent** none
Construction wired stems tightly bound with ribbon; decorated with wire and beads
Dress A-line, ballerina, empire-line

Sheaf Bouquet of Roses and Ivy

Flowers roses and leaves; ivy **Meaning** rose (red): happiness; ivy: fidelity, wedded love
Scent strong fragrance **Construction** hand-tied **Dress** A-line, column

Bouquet of Netted Roses

Flowers roses **Meaning** rose (red): happiness **Scent** strong fragrance
Construction hand-tied; decorated with beaded wire **Dress** A-line, column

Bouquet of Amaranthus and Gloriosas

Flowers amaranthus; gloriosas; ivy berries; chilli peppers; grasses; aspidistra leaves
Meaning amaranthus: immortality, unfading love; gloriosa: glorious beauty; ivy: fidelity, wedded love; grass: submission **Scent** none **Construction** wired stems bound on to a framework of reeds **Dress** ballerina, empire-line

Bouquet of Roses and Steel Grass

Flowers roses; steel grass **Meaning** rose (red): happiness; grass: submission
Scent strong fragrance **Construction** hand-tied **Dress** ballerina, empire-line

Formal Bouquet of Roses and Alchemilla

Flowers roses; *Alchemilla mollis*; galax leaves
Meaning rose (red): happiness; galax: encouragement **Scent** strong fragrance
Construction hand-tied; decorated with gold wire and glass beads
Dress ballerina, empire-line

Bouquet of Roses and Sea Holly

Flowers roses; sea holly; guelder rose; hosta leaves   **Meaning** rose (red): happiness
Scent strong fragrance   **Construction** hand-tied   **Dress** ballerina, empire-line

Bouquet of Tulips and Calla Lilies

Flowers tulips; calla lilies; leucadendron and camellia leaves
Meaning tulip: love, passion; calla lily: beauty **Scent** none **Construction** hand-tied
Dress ballerina, empire-line

Bouquet of Roses and Fern

Flowers roses; *Euphorbia martinii*; umbrella fern
Meaning rose (red): happiness; euphorbia: persistence; fern: sincerity
Scent strong fragrance **Construction** hand-tied **Dress** ballerina, empire-line

Bouquet of Roses and Galax Leaves

Flowers roses; cotoneaster berries; camellia and galax leaves
Meaning rose (red): happiness; camellia: admiration, perfection; galax: encouragement
Scent strong fragrance **Construction** wired stems bound into a handle and tied with ribbon
Dress ballerina, empire-line

Bouquet of Roses and Lilac

Flowers roses; lilac; freesias; celosias; bouvardia; hypericum berries; variegated and bear grasses **Meaning** rose (red): happiness; lilac: modesty, youthful innocence; freesia: friendship, innocence, trust; bouvardia: enthusiasm; grass: submission
Scent strong, sweet fragrance **Construction** hand-tied **Dress** ballerina, empire-line

Bouquet of Roses, Orchids and Ivy

Flowers roses; cymbidium orchids; ivy
Meaning rose (red): happiness; orchid: beauty, love, refinement; ivy: fidelity, wedded love
Scent strong fragrance **Construction** hand-tied **Dress** ballerina, empire-line

Shower Bouquet of Roses and Calla Lilies

Flowers roses; calla lilies; skimmia berries; bulrush leaves
Meaning rose (red): happiness; calla lily: beauty **Scent** strong fragrance
Construction wired stems bound into a sisal holder; decorated with gold wire
Dress A-line, column, mermaid

177

Pink

Trailing Bouquet of Orchids and Ivy

Flowers cymbidium orchids; bear grass; ivy
Meaning orchid: beauty, love, refinement; grass: submission; ivy: fidelity, wedded love
Scent slight fragrance **Construction** wired stems bound into a handle; decorated with pearl
beads **Dress** A-line, column

Informal Bouquet of Lilies and Grasses

Flowers lilies; bear grass; steel grass; monstera leaves
Meaning lily: purity of heart; grass: submission **Scent** strongly fragrant
Construction hand-tied **Dress** A-line, column, empire-line

Bouquet of Orchids

Flowers cymbidium orchids; bay leaves
Meaning orchid: beauty, love, refinement **Scent** none
Construction wired stems bound into a handle; decorated with diamanté
Dress ballerina, empire-line

Bouquet of Roses and Dracaena

Flowers roses; bronzed dracaena leaves **Meaning** rose (pale pink): grace, joy
Scent delicate fragrance **Construction** hand-tied; decorated with pearl beads
Dress ballerina, empire-line

Bouquet of Roses and Mint

Flowers roses; mint **Meaning** rose (pale pink): grace, joy;
rose (cream): innocence, purity; mint: virtue
Scent delicate fragrance **Construction** hand-tied
Dress ballerina, empire-line

Bouquet of Hydrangeas

Flowers hydrangeas; brachyglottis leaves **Meaning** hydrangea: thank you for understanding
Scent none **Construction** hand-tied **Dress** ballerina, empire-line

Bouquet of Tulips and Ruscus Leaves

Flowers parrot and double tulips; gypsophila; ruscus leaves
Meaning tulip: love, passion; gypsophila: innocence, purity of heart **Scent** slight fragrance
Construction hand-tied; decorated with silver wire and crystal beads
Dress ballerina, empire-line

Bouquet of Roses and Gerberas

Flowers roses; gerberas; salal leaves
Meaning rose (cream): innocence, purity; gerbera: innocence
Scent delicate fragrance   **Construction** hand-tied   **Dress** ballerina, empire-line

Rose Wand

Flowers roses; bamboo stems; copper beech leaves
Meaning rose (pale pink): grace, joy; beech: prosperity **Scent** none
Construction wired carmen rose; decorated with pearl beads **Dress** A-line, column

Bouquet of Roses

Flowers roses **Meaning** rose (pale pink): grace, joy **Scent** delicate fragrance
Construction hand-tied; wired crystal and pearl beads; decorated with silk tulle ribbon
Dress ballerina, empire-line

Shower Bouquet of Roses and Anthuriums

Flowers roses; anthuriums; tulips; cymbidium orchids; astilbes; milfoil; daylily and monstera leaves **Meaning** rose (white): innocence, purity; tulip: love, passion; orchid: beauty, love, refinement **Scent** slight fragrance
Construction wired stems bound into a handle **Dress** A-line, column

Shower Bouquet of Lilies and Roses

Flowers lilies; roses; gladioli; wax flowers; sedum; eucalyptus leaves
Meaning lily: purity of heart; rose (pale pink): grace, joy; gladiolus: generosity, sincerity
Scent strong, sweet fragrance **Construction** wired stems bound into a handle; decorated
with silk tulle **Dress** A-line, column

Bouquet of Roses and Ruscus

Flowers roses; ruscus and pittosporum leaves **Meaning** rose (pale pink): grace, joy
Scent slight fragrance **Construction** hand-tied **Dress** ballerina, empire-line

Shower Bouquet of Orchids and Calla Lilies

Flowers phalaenopsis orchids; calla lilies; daylily, monstera and galax leaves
Meaning orchid: beauty, love, refinement; calla lily: beauty; galax: encouragement
Scent none **Construction** wired stems bound into a handle **Dress** A-line, column, mermaid

Bouquet of Roses and Astilbes

Flowers roses; astilbes; calla lilies; bear grass; philodendron and phormium leaves
Meaning rose (pale pink): grace, joy; calla lily: beauty; grass: submission
Scent slight fragrance **Construction** hand-tied **Dress** A-line, column

Bouquet of Peonies and Calla Lilies

Flowers peonies; calla lilies; roses; celosias; sweet peas; rosemary; chive flowers; variegated grass **Meaning** peony: happy marriage; calla lily: beauty; rose (pale pink): grace, joy; sweet pea: blissful pleasure; grass: submission **Scent** strong, sweet fragrance **Construction** hand-tied **Dress** ballerina, empire-line

Bouquet of Peonies and Ivy

Flowers peonies; ivy and eucalyptus leaves
Meaning peony: happy marriage; ivy: fidelity, wedded love **Scent** strong fragrance
Construction hand-tied **Dress** A-line, column

Bouquet of Roses and Lavender

Flowers roses; lavender; *Euphorbia characias* and *Euphorbia griffithii*; hebe and sage leaves
Meaning rose (pink): perfect happiness; lavender: love, devotion; euphorbia: persistence
Scent slight fragrance **Construction** hand-tied **Dress** ballerina, empire-line

Formal Bouquet of Ranunculus

Flowers ranunculus **Meaning** ranunculus: charm, radiance
Scent none **Construction** hand-tied; wrapped in fabric **Dress** A-line, column

Bouquet of Lisianthus and Ranunculus

Flowers lisianthus; ranunculus; roses; guelder rose; brachyglottis leaves
Meaning ranunculus: charm, radiance; rose (pale pink): grace, joy
Scent slight fragrance **Construction** hand-tied **Dress** ballerina, empire-line

Trailing Bouquet of Calla Lilies and Roses

Flowers calla lilies; roses; dendrobium orchids; trachelium; bear grass
Meaning calla lily: beauty; rose (pink): perfect happiness; orchid: beauty, love, refinement;
grass: submission **Scent** sweet fragrance **Construction** wired stems bound into a handle;
decorated with gold wire **Dress** A-line, column, mermaid

Shower Bouquet of Roses and Hydrangeas

Flowers roses; hydrangeas; calla lilies; sedum; ivy
Meaning rose (pink): perfect happiness; hydrangea: thank you for understanding; calla lily:
beauty; ivy: fidelity, wedded love **Scent** slight fragrance **Construction** wired stems bound into
a handle; decorated with tulle ribbon and gold wire **Dress** A-line, column, mermaid

Bouquet of Roses and Laurustinus

Flowers roses; laurustinus **Meaning** rose (white):
innocence, purity; rose (pink): perfect happiness
Scent delicate, sweet fragrance **Construction** hand-tied; wrapped in tulle
Dress ballerina, empire-line

Wand of Anthuriums and Gemini Gerberas

Flowers anthuriums; germini gerberas; galax leaves
Meaning gerbera: innocence; galax: encouragement **Scent** none
Construction wired stems bound with ribbon **Dress** A-line, column

Column Bouquet of Orchids and Calla Lilies

Flowers cymbidium orchids; calla lilies; ranunculus; fern fronds; daylily and galax leaves
Meaning orchid: beauty, love, refinement; calla lily: beauty; ranunculus: charm, radiance; fern: sincerity; galax: encouragement **Scent** slight fragrance
Construction hand-tied; decorated with pearl beads **Dress** A-line, column

Bouquet of Roses

Flowers roses and rosebuds **Meaning** rose (pink): perfect happiness **Scent** slight fragrance
Construction hand-tied; decorated with ribbon and tulle **Dress** ballerina, empire-line

Bouquet of Roses and Astrantias

Flowers roses; astrantias; jasmine; eucalyptus
Meaning rose (pink): perfect happiness; jasmine: amiability **Scent** strong, sweet fragrance
Construction hand-tied **Dress** ballerina, empire-line

Bouquet of Orchids and Roses

Flowers cymbidium orchids; roses; steel grass; aspidistra and salal leaves
Meaning orchid: beauty, love, refinement; rose (pink): perfect happiness; grass: submission
Scent warm, sweet fragrance **Construction** hand-tied **Dress** ballerina, column, empire-line

Bridal Wand of Nerines and Orchids

Flowers nerines; cymbidium and dendrobium orchids; sweetheart vine; bear grass; asparagus fern; dracaena leaves **Meaning** orchid: beauty, love, refinement **Scent** none
Construction wired stems bound with ribbon into a handle; decorated with pearlized beads
Dress A-line, column

Bouquet of Anthuriums and Orchids

Flowers anthuriums; phalaenopsis orchids; steel grass; ivy; aspidistra leaves
Meaning orchid: beauty, love, refinement; grass: submission; ivy: fidelity, wedded love
Scent none **Construction** hand-tied **Dress** A-line, column

Informal Bouquet of Agapanthus and Roses

Flowers agapanthus seedhead; roses; paphiopedilum orchids; sea holly; bear grass
Meaning rose (pink): perfect happiness; orchid: beauty, love, refinement; grass: submission
Scent slight fragrance **Construction** hand-tied with raffia and twigs **Dress** column, empire-line

Bouquet of Veronica and Alstroemerias

Flowers veronica; alstroemeria; roses; carnations; galax leaves
Meaning veronica: fidelity; alstroemeria: fortune, prosperity, wealth; rose (pink): perfect
happiness; carnation: devoted love, fascination; galax: encouragement
Scent warm, spicy fragrance **Construction** hand-tied **Dress** ballerina, empire-line

Posy of Roses and Hydrangeas

Flowers roses; hydrangeas; calla lilies; lisianthus; variegated grass; hosta leaves
Meaning rose (pink): perfect happiness; hydrangea: thank you for
understanding; calla lily: beauty; grass: submission **Scent** slight fragrance
Construction hand-tied **Dress** ballerina, empire-line

Posy of Roses

Flowers roses **Meaning** rose (pink): perfect happiness **Scent** slight fragrance
Construction hand-tied **Dress** ballerina, empire-line

Bouquet of Roses and Hydrangeas

Flowers roses; hydrangeas; salal leaves
Meaning rose (pale pink): grace, joy; hydrangea: thank you for understanding
Scent slight fragrance **Construction** hand-tied; decorated with gold wire and pearl beads
Dress ballerina, empire-line

Bouquet of Alliums and Ranunculus

Flowers alliums; ranunculus; roses; parrot tulips; bupleurum leaves
Meaning ranunculus: charm, radiance; rose (pink): perfect happiness; tulip: love, passion
Scent strong fragrance **Construction** hand-tied **Dress** ballerina, empire-line

Bouquet of Celosias and Calla Lilies

Flowers celosias; calla lilies; roses; bear grass; fern fronds; cordyline and hebe leaves
Meaning calla lily: beauty; rose (pink): perfect happiness; grass: submission; fern: sincerity
Scent delicate fragrance **Construction** hand-tied; decorated with pearl beads
Dress ballerina, empire-line

Freestyle Bouquet of Orchids

Flowers cymbidium orchids; equisetum **Meaning** orchid: beauty, love, refinement **Scent** none
Construction wired stems bound into a handle **Dress** A-line, column

Trailing Bouquet of Roses and Tulips

Flowers roses; parrot tulips; calla lilies; trailing succulent; grass; galax leaves
Meaning rose (pink): perfect happiness; tulip: love, passion; calla lily: beauty; grass: submission; galax: encouragement **Scent** slight fragrance **Construction** wired stems bound into a handle; decorated with silver wire and crystal beads **Dress** ballerina, empire-line

Bouquet of Roses and Statice

Flowers roses; statice; sea holly; lilies; calla lilies
Meaning rose (pink): perfect happiness; lily: purity of heart; calla lily: beauty
Scent slight fragrance **Construction** wired stems bound into a handle; decorated with red wire
Dress ballerina, empire-line

Posy of Orchids and Roses

Flowers cymbidium orchids; roses; hypericum berries; *Brunia albiflora*; eucalyptus leaves
Meaning orchid: beauty, love, refinement; rose (pink): perfect happiness **Scent** slight fragrance
Construction hand-tied **Dress** ballerina, empire-line

Bouquet of Roses and Cestrum

Flowers roses; cestrum; ranunculus; hellebores; galax leaves; trailing succulent
Meaning rose (pink): perfect happiness; ranunculus: charm, radiance; galax: encouragement
Scent sweet fragrance **Construction** wired stems bound into a handle;
decorated with silver wire and crystal beads **Dress** A-line, ballerina

Freestyle Bouquet of Lily-of-the-valley and Roses

Flowers lily-of-the-valley; roses; ivy
Meaning lily-of-the-valley: return of happiness; rose (pink): perfect happiness; ivy:
fidelity, wedded love **Scent** strong, sweet fragrance **Construction** hand-tied;
decorated with wired freshwater pearls **Dress** A-line, column, mermaid

Formal Bouquet of Roses and Ranunculus

Flowers roses; ranunculus; lisianthus

Meaning rose (pink): perfect happiness; ranunculus: charm, radiance **Scent** slight fragrance

Construction hand-tied; decorated with silver wire **Dress** ballerina, empire-line

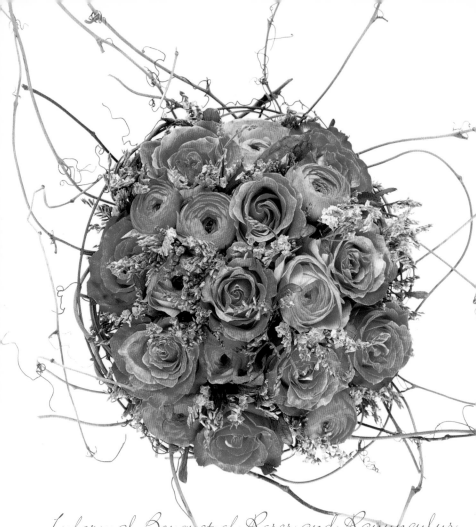

Informal Bouquet of Roses and Ranunculus

Flowers roses; ranunculus; statice; willow
Meaning rose (pink): perfect happiness; ranunculus: charm, radiance
Scent sweet fragrance **Construction** wired stems bound into a handle
Dress ballerina, empire-line

Bouquet of Hippeastrums

Flowers hippeastrums **Meaning** hippeastrum: expectation, splendid beauty **Scent** none
Construction wired stems bound into a handle; decorated with wired crystal beads
Dress ballerina, empire-line

Bouquet of Lisianthus and Calla Lilies

Flowers lisianthus; calla lilies; lilac; statice; asparagus fern
Meaning calla lily: beauty; lilac: first emotion of love; asparagus fern: fascination
Scent strong, sweet fragrance **Construction** wired stems tightly bound
into a cone; decorated with silver wire **Dress** A-line, column

Bouquet of Roses and Celosias

Flowers roses; celosias; hydrangeas
Meaning rose (pale pink): grace, joy; hydrangea: thank you for understanding
Scent slight fragrance **Construction** hand-tied **Dress** ballerina, empire-line

Bouquet of Calla Lilies, Roses and Berries

Flowers calla lilies; roses; viburnum berries; bear grass; ruscus leaves
Meaning calla lily: beauty; rose (pale pink): grace, joy; grass: submission
Scent slight fragrance **Construction** wired stems bound into a handle
Dress ballerina, empire-line

Bouquet of Irises and Roses

Flowers irises; roses; lisianthus; rosemary; hypericum berries; hebe, pittosporum and anthurium leaves **Meaning** iris: faith, hope, wisdom; rose (pink): perfect happiness **Scent** slight fragrance **Construction** hand-tied; decorated gold wire **Dress** ballerina, empire-line

Over-arm Bouquet of Calla Lilies and Grass

Flowers calla lilies; steel and bear grasses; hosta leaves
Meaning calla lily: beauty; grass: submission **Scent** none
Construction wired stems bound into a handle; decorated with glass beads
Dress A-line, column, mermaid

Formal Bouquet of Roses and Beads

Flowers roses **Meaning** rose (pink): perfect happiness **Scent** slight fragrance
Construction wired stems bound into a handle; decorated with silver wire and crystal beads
Dress ballerina, empire-line

Shower Bouquet of Lilies and Roses

Flowers lilies; roses; hydrangeas; snowberries; daylily leaves
Meaning lily: purity of heart; rose (pink): perfect happiness; hydrangea:
thank you for understanding **Scent** strong, sweet fragrance
Construction wired stems bound into a handle **Dress** A-line, column

Tear-drop Bouquet of Calla Lilies and Grass

Flowers calla lilies; variegated grass **Meaning** calla lily: beauty; grass: submission
Scent none **Construction** wired stems bound into a handle **Dress** A-line, column

Informal Bouquet of Roses and Aspidistra Leaves

Flowers roses; bronzed aspidistra leaves **Meaning** rose (pink): perfect happiness
Scent slight fragrance **Construction** wired stems bound into a handle **Dress** A-line, column

Crescent Bouquet of Anthuriums

Flowers anthuriums; calla lilies; laurustinus; leucadendrons; bear grass; milfoil
Meaning calla lily: beauty; grass: submission **Scent** none
Construction wired stems bound into a handle **Dress** A-line, column, mermaid

Bouquet of Protea and Roses

Flowers protea; roses; hypericum berries; hyacinths; aspidistra leaves
Meaning rose (pink): perfect happiness; hyacinth: playful joy **Scent** strong, sweet fragrance
Construction hand-tied; decorated with feathers **Dress** ballerina, empire-line

Bouquet of Calla Lilies and Bouvardia

Flowers calla lilies; bouvardia; roses; eucalyptus and fatsia leaves
Meaning calla lily: beauty; bouvardia: enthusiasm; rose (pink): perfect happiness
Scent strong, sweet fragrance **Construction** hand-tied **Dress** ballerina, empire-line

Bouquet of Astilbes and Roses

Flowers astilbes; roses **Meaning** rose (white): innocence, purity; rose (pink): perfect happiness
Scent strong fragrance **Construction** hand-tied **Dress** ballerina, empire-line

Bouquet of Orchids, Roses and Ivy

Flowers cymbidium orchids; roses; ivy berries
Meaning orchid: beauty, love, refinement; rose (pink): perfect happiness;
rose (red): happiness; ivy: fidelity, wedded love   **Scent** strongly fragrant
Construction hand-tied   **Dress** ballerina, empire-line

Bouquet of Roses and Anthuriums

Flowers roses; anthuriums; bear grass; cordyline leaves
Meaning rose (pink): perfect happiness; grass: submission **Scent** sweet fragrance
Construction hand-tied with ribbon **Dress** ballerina, empire-line

Trailing Bouquet of Calla Lilies and Roses

Flowers calla lilies; roses; clematis stems; hydrangeas; *Brunia albiflora*; steel grass
Meaning calla lily: beauty; clematis: ingenuity; hydrangea: thank you for understanding; rose: (pink) perfect happiness; grass: submission **Scent** slight fragrance
Construction wired stems bound into a handle **Dress** A-line, column

Bouquet of Nerines and Gerberas

Flowers nerines; gerberas; roses; cymbidium orchids; amaranthus; ixias; miscanthus; cordyline, salal and palm leaves **Meaning** gerbera: innocence; rose (pink): perfect happiness; orchid: beauty, love; amaranthus: unfading love; grass: submission; palm: success **Scent** slight fragrance **Construction** hand-tied; decorated with pink wire **Dress** ballerina, empire-line

Bouquet of Orchids and Astrantias

Flowers cymbidium orchids; astrantias; hypericum berries; bear grass
Meaning orchid: beauty, love, refinement; grass: submission **Scent** none
Construction hand-tied; encased in a framework of willow stems **Dress** ballerina, empire-line

Bouquet of Nerines and Calla Lilies

Flowers nerines; calla lilies; roses **Meaning** calla lily: beauty; rose (red): happiness
Scent strong fragrance **Construction** hand-tied **Dress** A-line, column

Bouquet of Gloriosas and Roses

Flowers gloriosas; roses; ruscus and cordyline leaves
Meaning gloriosa: glorious beauty; rose (pink): perfect happiness; rose
(deep pink): thankfulness **Scent** strong fragrance
Construction hand-tied; decorated with wired pearl beads **Dress** ballerina, empire-line

Bouquet of Orchids and Celosias

Flowers vanda orchids; celosias; daylily leaves **Meaning** orchid: beauty, love, refinement
Scent none **Construction** hand-tied **Dress** A-line, column

Bouquet of Freesias and Birch

Flowers freesias; ivy; steel grass; holly, fatsia and palm leaves; birch twigs
Meaning freesia: friendship, innocence, trust; grass: submission; palm: success, victory; birch: elegance, grace, meekness **Scent** strong, sweet fragrance **Construction** wired stems bound with sisal; decorated with silver wire and wired pine needles **Dress** A-line, column, mermaid

247

Bouquet of Gerberas and Tulips

Flowers gerberas; tulips; aspidistra leaves **Meaning** gerbera: innocence; tulip: love, passion
Scent none **Construction** hand-tied; decorated with silver wire and wired pearl beads
Dress ballerina, empire-line

Bouquet of Gerberas and Calla Lilies

Flowers germini gerberas; calla lilies; roses; celosias; guelder rose; hypericum berries
Meaning gerbera: innocence; calla lily: beauty; rose (pink): perfect happiness; rose (red):
happiness **Scent** slight, sweet fragrance **Construction** wired stems bound into a handle;
decorated with gold wire **Dress** ballerina, empire-line

Tear-drop Bouquet of Calla Lilies and Roses

Flowers calla lilies; roses; sedum; celosias; moluccella; alstroemerias; astrantias, lisianthus; hydrangeas; leycesteria; heather; pepper berries; pittosporum and hebe leaves **Meaning** calla lily: beauty; rose: happiness; moluccella: good luck; hydrangea: thanks for understanding **Scent** slight fragrance **Construction** wired stems bound into a handle **Dress** ballerina, empire-line

Trailing Bouquet of Anthuriums and Orchids

Flowers anthuriums; cymbidium orchids; bear grass; phormium and monstera leaves
Meaning orchid: beauty, love, refinement; grass: submission **Scent** none
Construction stems wired and bound into a handle **Dress** A-line, column

Bouquet of Roses and Ranunculus

Flowers roses; ranunculus; tulips; freesias; ruscus leaves
Meaning rose (deep pink): thankfulness; ranunculus: charm, radiance; tulips: love,
passion; freesia: friendship, innocence, trust **Scent** strong fragrance
Construction hand-tied; decorated with feathers **Dress** ballerina, empire-line

Informal Bouquet of Roses and Ivy

Flowers roses; ivy leaves and berries
Meaning rose (deep pink): thankfulness; ivy: fidelity, wedded love   **Scent** sweet fragrance
Construction hand-tied; decorated with gold beads   **Dress** A-line, column

Bouquet of Spray Roses and Grass

Flowers roses; bear grass **Meaning** rose (deep pink): thankfulness; grass: submission
Scent strong fragrance **Construction** hand-tied **Dress** ballerina, empire-line

Bouquet of Roses and Viburnum Berries

Flowers roses; viburnum berries; rosemary; ivy
Meaning rose (deep pink): thankfulness; rosemary: remembrance; ivy: fidelity, wedded love
Scent sweet fragrance **Construction** hand-tied **Dress** ballerina, empire-line

Trailing Bouquet of Orchids

Flowers cymbidium orchids; jasmine stems; sweetheart vine; bear grass; hebe, aspidistra and beaucarnea leaves **Meaning** orchid: beauty, love, refinement; jasmine: amiability; grass: submission **Scent** slight fragrance **Construction** wired stems bound with tulle ribbon **Dress** A-line, column

Wrist Bouquet of Gerberas and Ruscus

Flowers germini gerberas; bear grass; ruscus leaves
Meaning gerbera: innocence; grass: submission **Scent** none
Construction wired stems bound to form a wristlet **Dress** A-line, column, mermaid

Dome Bouquet of Roses

Flowers roses **Meaning** rose (deep pink): thankfulness **Scent** slight fragrance
Construction wired stems bound into a handle **Dress** ballerina, empire-line

Shower Bouquet of Calla Lilies and Nerines

Flowers calla lilies; nerines; roses; astilbes **Meaning** calla lily: beauty; rose (red): happiness
Scent strong fragrance **Construction** wired stems bound into a handle **Dress** A-line, column

Posy of Roses and Calla Lilies

Flowers roses; calla lilies; ivy berries
Meaning rose (deep pink): thankfulness; rose (red): happiness; calla lily: beauty; ivy: fidelity, wedded love **Scent** strong fragrance **Construction** hand-tied **Dress** ballerina, empire-line

Bouquet of Calla Lilies and Asclepias

Flowers calla lilies; asclepias; roses; eucalyptus leaves
Meaning calla lily: beauty; rose (deep pink): thankfulness **Scent** slight fragrance
Construction wired stems bound into a handle **Dress** A-line, column

Bouquet of Three Roses

Flowers roses Meaning rose (pink): perfect happiness; rose (deep pink):
thankfulness; rose (red): happiness Scent strong fragrance
Construction hand-tied Dress A-line, empire-line, column

Posy of Lilies and Roses

Flowers lilies; roses; poppy seedheads; hypericum berries; ivy leaves and berries; birch twigs
Meaning lily: purity of heart; rose (pink): perfect happiness; ivy: fidelity, wedded love;
birch: elegance, grace, meekness **Scent** slight fragrance
Construction hand-tied **Dress** ballerina, empire-line

Lilac and Purple

Bouquet of Gypsophila and Calla Lilies

Flowers gypsophila; calla lilies; statice
Meaning gypsophila: innocence, purity of heart; calla lily: beauty
Scent none **Construction** hand-tied **Dress** ballerina, empire-line

Bouquet of Lilac

Flowers lilac **Meaning** lilac (white): modesty, youthful innocence; lilac (purple): first emotion of love
Scent strong, sweet fragrance **Construction** hand-tied with tulle ribbon **Dress** A-line, column

Bouquet of Roses and Hyacinths

Flowers roses; hyacinths; freesias; lisianthus; variegated grass; ivy, galax and salal leaves
Meaning rose (pale pink): grace, joy; hyacinth: playful joy; freesia: friendship, innocence, trust;
grass: submission; galax: encouragement; ivy: fidelity, wedded love **Scent** strong
fragrance **Construction** wired stems bound into a handle **Dress** ballerina, empire-line

Bouquet of Roses and Hyacinths

Flowers roses; hyacinths; hebe leaves
Meaning rose (pale pink): grace, joy; hyacinth: playful joy **Scent** strong, sweet fragrance
Construction hand-tied and decorated with ribbon **Dress** ballerina, empire-line

Crescent Bouquet of Freesias and Delphiniums

Flowers freesias; delphiniums; agapanthus; scabious; lilac; laurustinus berries; bear grass; aspidistra leaves **Meaning** freesia: friendship, innocence, trust; delphinium: ardent attachment; lilac: modesty, youthful innocence; grass: submission **Scent** strong, sweet fragrance **Construction** wired stems bound into a handle **Dress** A-line, column

Bouquet of Lisianthus and Chrysanthemums

Flowers lisianthus; chrysanthemums; roses; freesias; variegated grass; daylily and salal leaves; passionflower stems **Meaning** chrysanthemum: truth; rose (pink): perfect happiness; freesia: friendship, innocence, trust; grass: submission **Scent** strong, sweet fragrance **Construction** hand-tied **Dress** ballerina, empire-line

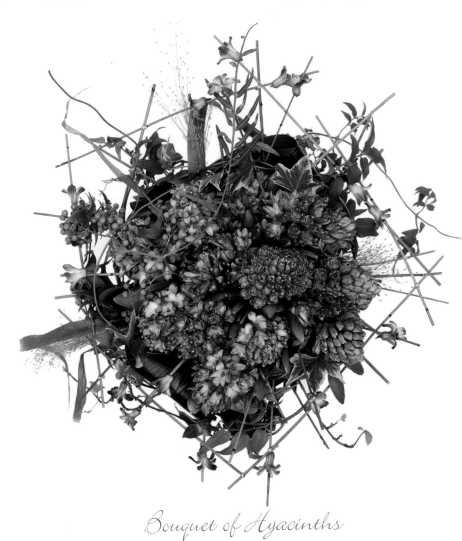

Bouquet of Hyacinths

Flowers hyacinths; pepper berries; miscanthus; jasmine, ivy and aspidistra leaves
Meaning hyacinth: playful joy; grass: submission; jasmine: amiability; ivy: fidelity, wedded love
Scent sweet fragrance **Construction** hand-tied to a frame of reeds
Dress ballerina, empire-line

Bouquet of Orchids and Freesia Petals

Flowers vanda orchids; freesias; bear grass
Meaning orchid: beauty, love, refinement; freesia: friendship, innocence, trust; grass: submission
Scent slight fragrance **Construction** wired stems bound into a handle; decorated with diamanté beads **Dress** A-line, column, mermaid

Bouquet of Anthuriums and Lisianthus

Flowers anthuriums; lisianthus; roses; freesias; ivy and bronzed cordyline leaves
Meaning rose (pale pink): grace, joy; freesia: friendship, innocence,
trust; ivy: fidelity, wedded love **Scent** sweet, subtle fragrance
Construction hand-tied **Dress** A-line, column

Bouquet of Delphiniums and Hydrangeas

Flowers delphiniums; hydrangeas; asparagus fern; passionflower stems; ivy leaves
Meaning delphinium: ardent attachment; hydrangea: thank you for understanding; asparagus
fern: fascination **Scent** none **Construction** hand-tied **Dress** A-line, column

Bouquet of Liatris and Lisianthus

Flowers liatris; lisianthus; freesias; sea holly; phlox; veronicas; ruscus, aspidistra and eucalyptus leaves **Meaning** freesia: friendship, innocence, trust; phlox: unity; veronica: fidelity **Scent** strong, sweet fragrance **Construction** hand-tied **Dress** ballerina, empire-line

Bouquet of Anemones and Leucadendrons

Flowers anemones; leucadendrons; roses; hypericum berries; ornamental brassicas; daylily leaves **Meaning** anemone: expectation; rose (pink): perfect happiness
Scent slight fragrance **Construction** hand-tied **Dress** ballerina, empire-line

Bouquet of Orchids and Bassia

Flowers vanda orchids; bassia; roses; privet berries; bear grass; ficus leaves
Meaning orchid: beauty, love, refinement; rose (pink): perfect happiness; grass: submission
Scent slight fragrance **Construction** wired stems bound into a handle **Dress** A-line, column

Trailing Bouquet of Delphiniums and Freesias

Flowers delphiniums; freesias; lisianthus; veronicas; laurustinus berries; steel
and variegated grasses; setaria seedheads; fatsia and eucalyptus leaves; skeletonized leaves
Meaning delphinium: ardent attachment; freesia: friendship, innocence, trust; veronica: fidelity;
grass: submission **Scent** sweet fragrance **Construction** wired stems **Dress** A-line, column

Bouquet of Irises and Gypsophila

Flowers irises; gypsophila; hyacinth bells
Meaning iris: faith, hope, wisdom; gypsophila: innocence, purity of heart; hyacinth: playful joy
Scent slight fragrance **Construction** wired stems bound into a handle; decorated with gold wire
Dress ballerina, empire-line

Tear-drop Bouquet of Roses and Lisianthus

Flowers roses; lisianthus; sweet peas; guelder rose; ruscus leaves
Meaning rose (mauve): happiness; sweet pea: blissful pleasure **Scent** strong, sweet fragrance
Construction wired stems bound into a handle; decorated with silver wire and pearl beads
Dress A-line, column

Bouquet of Freesias and Roses

Flowers freesias; roses; statice; bear grass; eucalyptus leaves
Meaning freesia: friendship, innocence, trust; rose (mauve): happiness; grass: submission
Scent strong, sweet fragrance **Construction** hand-tied **Dress** ballerina, empire-line

Bouquet of Sweet Peas and Hydrangeas

Flowers sweet peas; hydrangeas; freesias; veronicas; anemones
Meaning sweet pea: blissful pleasure; hydrangea: thank you for understanding;
freesia: friendship, innocence, trust; veronica: fidelity; anemone: expectation
Scent strong, sweet fragrance **Construction** hand-tied **Dress** ballerina, empire-line

Nosegay of Lavender and Alliums

Flowers lavender; alliums; rosemary; sage leaves
Meaning lavender: love, devotion; rosemary: remembrance **Scent** strong fragrance
Construction wired stems bound into a handle; decorated with fabric and gold wire
Dress A-line, column

Trailing Bouquet of Hyacinths and Alliums

Flowers hyacinths; alliums; thistles; lisianthus; eucalyptus leaves
Meaning hyacinth: playful joy **Scent** strong, sweet fragrance
Construction wired stems bound into a handle; decorated with sisal, wire and crystal beads
Dress A-line, empire-line

Bouquet of Orchids, Calla Lilies and Grass

Flowers vanda orchids; calla lilies; steel grass; autumn eucalyptus and aspidistra leaves
Meaning orchid: beauty, love, refinement; calla lily: beauty; grass: submission
Scent none **Construction** wired stems bound into a handle
Dress ballerina, empire-line

Bouquet of Lisianthus and Fern Fronds

Flowers lisianthus; anemones; mokara orchids; freesias; tulips; umbrella fern
Meaning anemone: expectation; orchid: beauty, love, refinement; freesia: friendship,
innocence, trust: tulip: love, passion; fern: sincerity **Scent** strong, sweet fragrance
Construction hand-tied **Dress** ballerina, empire-line

287

Shower Bouquet of Orchids and Grass

Flowers vanda orchids; bear grass; asparagus fern
Meaning orchid: beauty, love, refinement; grass: submission: asparagus fern: fascination
Scent none **Construction** wired stems bound into a handle; decorated with pearl beads
Dress A-line, column, mermaid

Bouquet of Anemones

Flowers anemones, brassica hearts; hypericum berries; asplenium leaves
Meaning anemone: expectation; fern: sincerity **Scent** none
Construction hand-tied **Dress** ballerina, empire-line

Bouquet of Irises

Flowers irises; monstera leaf **Meaning** iris: faith, hope, wisdom **Scent** none
Construction hand-tied; decorated with gold wire and pearl beads
Dress ballerina, empire-line

Bouquet of Ranunculus and African Violets

Flowers ranunculus; African violets; anemones; skimmia; campanulas; phlox
Meaning ranunculus: charm, radiance; anemone: expectation
Scent none **Construction** hand-tied **Dress** ballerina, empire-line

Bouquet of Agapanthus and Calla Lilies

Flowers agapanthus; calla lilies; anemones; hyacinths; statice
Meaning calla lily: beauty; anemone: expectation; hyacinth: playful joy
Scent strong, sweet fragrance **Construction** wired stems bound into a handle
Dress ballerina, empire-line

Dome Bouquet of Orchids

Flowers vanda orchids **Meaning** orchid: beauty, love, refinement **Scent** none
Construction wired stems bound into a handle **Dress** ballerina, empire-line

Bouquet of Lisianthus and Mint

Flowers lisianthus; mint **Meaning** mint: virtue **Scent** strong, herby fragrance
Construction hand-tied **Dress** ballerina; empire-line

Bouquet of Muscaris and Anemones

Flowers muscaris; anemones; lisianthus; laurustinus berries **Meaning** anemone: expectation
Scent none **Construction** hand-tied **Dress** ballerina, empire-line

Mixed and Unusual

Bouquet of Roses and Sweet Peas

Flowers roses; sweet peas; hypericum berries
Meaning rose (cream): innocence, purity; sweet pea: blissful pleasure **Scent** strong fragrance
Construction wired stems bound into a handle **Dress** ballerina, empire-line

Bouquet of Chrysanthemums and Gerberas

Flowers chrysanthemums; gerberas; freesias; lisianthus; leucadendrons; roses; ranunculus; hypericum berries **Meaning** chrysanthemum: truth; gerbera: innocence; freesia: friendship, innocence, trust; rose (cream): innocence, purity; ranunculus: charm, radiance **Scent** strong, sweet fragrance **Construction** wired stems bound into a handle **Dress** ballerina, empire-line

Bouquet of Lilies and Anthuriums

Flowers *Lilium longiflorum*; anthuriums; roses; cymbidium orchids; rosemary; rhipsalis; hypericum berries; jasmine stems; hebe and phormium leaves **Meaning** lily: modesty, purity; rose (white): innocence, purity; orchid: beauty, love, refinement; rosemary: remembrance; jasmine: amiability **Scent** strong fragrance **Construction** hand-tied **Dress** ballerina, empire-line

Bouquet of Calla Lilies and Umbrella Fern

Flowers calla lilies; agapanthus; umbrella fern **Meaning** calla lily: beauty; fern: sincerity
Scent none **Construction** hand-tied **Dress** ballerina, empire-line

Bouquet of Celosias and Roses

Flowers celosias; roses; freesias; salal and aspidistra leaves
Meaning rose (green): friendship, joy; freesia: friendship, innocence, trust
Scent sweet fragrance **Construction** hand-tied **Dress** ballerina, empire-line

Bouquet of Hydrangeas and Sedum

Flowers hydrangeas; sedum; bouvardia; calla lilies; roses
Meaning hydrangea: thank you for understanding; bouvardia: enthusiasm; calla lily: beauty;
rose (cream): innocence, purity **Scent** sweet fragrance **Construction** hand-tied
Dress ballerina, empire-line

Bouquet of Carnations and Foliage

Flowers carnations; poppy seedheads; pine cones and needles; aspidistra, mahonia and skimmia leaves; azalea twigs **Meaning** carnation: devoted love, fascination; pine: hope **Scent** warm, spicy fragrance **Construction** hand-tied **Dress** ballerina, empire-line

Formal Bouquet of Roses

Flowers roses **Meaning** rose (cream): innocence, purity; rose
(pale pink): grace, joy; rose (red): happiness **Scent** strong fragrance
Construction wired stems bound into a handle; decorated with wire
Dress ballerina, empire-line

Bouquet of Ranunculus and Guelder Rose

Flowers ranunculus; guelder rose; lisianthus; roses
Meaning ranunculus: charm, radiance; rose (pink): perfect happiness
Scent slight fragrance **Construction** hand-tied and bound with ribbon
Dress A-line, empire-line

Ball Bouquet of Roses

Flowers roses; pittosporum leaves
Meaning rose (white): innocence, purity; rose (deep pink): thankfulness **Scent** slight fragrance
Construction wired stems; decorated with pearl beads **Dress** ballerina, empire-line

Bouquet of Roses and Cornflowers

Flowers roses; cornflowers; rosemary
Meaning rose (green): friendship, joy; cornflower: delicacy, refinement; rosemary: remembrance
Scent slight fragrance **Construction** hand-tied **Dress** ballerina, empire-line

Bouquet of Gloriosas and Calla Lilies

Flowers gloriosas; calla lilies; roses; steel grass; fatsia leaves **Meaning** gloriosa:
glorious beauty; calla lily: beauty; rose (yellow): friendship, joy; grass: submission
Scent slight fragrance / **Construction** hand-tied with ribbon; decorated with gold jewellery
Dress A-line, column

Bouquet of Peonies and Bluebells

Flowers peonies; bluebells; roses; eucalyptus leaves
Meaning peony: happy marriage; bluebell: constancy; rose (yellow): friendship, joy
Scent sweet fragrance **Construction** hand-tied **Dress** ballerina, empire-line

Bouquet of Gerberas and Celosias

Flowers gerberas; celosias; roses; palm leaves
Meaning gerbera: innocence; rose (pink): perfect happiness; rose (orange): desire,
enthusiasm, fascination; palm: success, victory **Scent** slight fragrance
Construction wired stems bound into a handle **Dress** A-line, column

Bouquet of Tulips and Anemones

Flowers tulips; anemones; lotus seedheads; variegated grass; salal leaves
Meaning tulip: love, passion; anemone: expectation; grass: submission
Scent none **Construction** hand-tied **Dress** ballerina, empire-line

Bouquet of Peonies and Celosias

Flowers peonies; celosias; calla lilies; roses; euphorbia; bouvardia
Meaning peony: happy marriage; calla lily: beauty; rose (red): happiness; bouvardia:
enthusiasm **Scent** slight fragrance **Construction** hand-tied **Dress** ballerina, empire-line

Posy of Brassica and Chrysanthemums

Flowers brassicas; chrysanthemums; steel grass
Meaning chrysanthemum: truth; grass: submission **Scent** none
Construction wired stems bound into a handle; decorated with beads and sisal
Dress ballerina, empire-line

Bouquet of Grasses and Carnation Petals

Flowers carnations; bear grass
Meaning carnation: devoted love, fascination; grass: submission **Scent** faint, spicy fragrance
Construction wired grasses decorated with individual carnation petals
Dress A-line, column, mermaid

Fan of Lilies and Fatsia Leaves

Flowers *Lilium longiflorum*; fatsia and galax leaves
Meaning lily: modesty, purity; galax: encouragement **Scent** very strong fragrance
Construction wired and bound with ribbon; decorated with wired pearl beads
Dress A-line, ballerina, empire-line

Fan of Roses and Box Leaves

Flowers roses; asparagus fern; box leaves
Meaning rose (white): innocence, purity; asparagus fern: fascination; box: constancy
Scent none **Construction** wired stems; decorated with pearl beads **Dress** A-line, empire-line

Fan of Craspedia and Calla Lilies

Flowers craspedia; calla lilies; oncidium and cymbidium orchids; bear grass; palm leaves
Meaning calla lily: beauty; orchid: beauty, love, refinement; grass: submission; palm: success,
victory **Scent** slight, sweet fragrance **Construction** wired stems tightly bound in ribbon;
decorated with gold wire **Dress** A-line, column

Basket of Roses in Gold Wire

Flowers roses; tulip leaves **Meaning** rose (orange): desire, enthusiasm, fascination
Scent slight fragrance **Construction** wired stems arranged in a sisal basket
Dress ballerina, empire-line

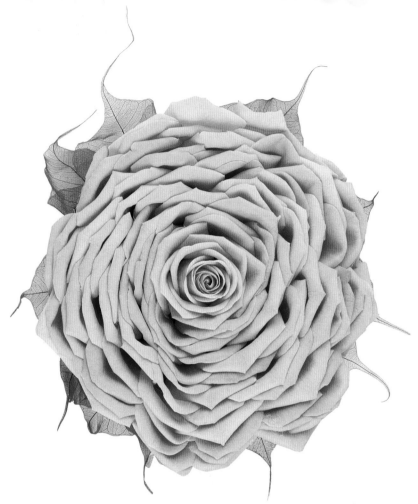

Carmen Rose and Skeletonized Leaves

Flowers carmen rose; skeletonized leaves **Meaning** rose (pink): perfect happiness
Scent none **Construction** wired carmen rose **Dress** ballerina, empire-line

Basket of Roses

Flowers roses; carnation petals
Meaning rose (pink): perfect happiness; carnation: devoted love, fascination **Scent** slight
Construction basket covered with carnation petals and decorated with feathers
Dress ballerina, empire-line

Fan of Orchids

Flowers dendrobium orchids; palm fronds
Meaning orchid: beauty, love, refinement; palm: success, victory **Scent** none
Construction wired stems bound into a handle; decorated with feathers **Dress** A-line, column

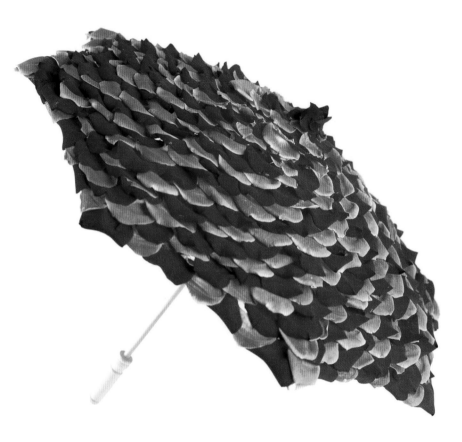

Parasol Decorated with Rose Petals

Flowers roses **Meaning** rose (pink): perfect happiness; rose (red): happiness
Scent none **Construction** individually wired petals
Dress ballerina, empire-line

Heart-shaped Bouquet of Orchids and Grass

Flowers cymbidium orchids; bear grass
Meaning orchid: beauty, love, refinement; grass: submission **Scent** none
Construction wired stems bound into a framework of cornus stems **Dress** A-line, column

Heart-shaped Bouquet of Roses

Flowers roses **Meaning** rose (red): happiness **Scent** strong fragrance
Construction wired stems bound into sisal heart surrounding red glass heart
Dress ballerina, empire-line

Carmen Rose and Crystal Beads

Flowers carmen rose; galax leaves
Meaning carmen rose (red): happiness; galax: encouragement **Scent** strong fragrance
Construction wired carmen rose decorated with gold wire and crystal beads
Dress ballerina, empire-line

Handbag of Roses

Flowers roses **Meaning** rose (red): happiness **Scent** slight fragrance
Construction roses arranged in oasis; decorated with diamanté brooch **Dress** column

Common Flower Names

The following list includes the common names of the flowers and shrubs illustrated in this book only when the botanical name differs markedly from the common name and when it might be difficult or confusing to identify the particular plants you would like to include in your wedding flowers. Common names can vary not only from country to country but also from area to area within countries, so make sure that you and your florist have the same flower in mind when you are making your plans.

Common name	Botanical name	Common name	Botanical name
African violet	*Saintpaulia* spp.	lisianthus	*Eustoma grandiflorum*
bear grass	*Xerophyllum tenax*	lotus	*Nelumbo* spp.
birch	*Betula* spp.	love grass	*Eragrostis* spp.
bulrush	*Typha* spp.	Queen Anne's lace	*Anthriscus sylvestris*
calla lily	*Zantedeschia* spp.	salal	*Gaultheria shallon*
chincherinchees	*Ornithogalum thyrsoides*	sea holly	*Eryngium* spp.
croton	*Codiaeum* spp.	snowberry	*Symphoricarpos albus*
daylily	*Hemerocallis* spp.		var. *laevigatus*
fountain grass	*Pennisetum* spp.	statice	*Limonium* spp. (sea
galax	*Galax urceolata* (wand-		lavender)
	flower)	steel grass	*Phalaris* or *Stipa* spp.
globe thistle	*Echinops* spp.	sunflower	*Helianthus annuus*
gloriosa	*Gloriosa superba* (glory	sweetheart vine	*Ceropegia linearis* subsp.
	lily)		*woodii* (hearts on a
guelder rose	*Viburnum opulus*		string, rosary vine)
holly	*Ilex* spp.	sweet pea	*Lathyrus odoratus*
ivy	*Hedera* spp.	tea tree	*Leptospermum lanigerum*
kangaroo paw	*Anigozanthos* spp.	umbrella fern	*Sticherus cunninghamii*
laurustinus	*Viburnum tinus*	wax flower	*Hoya* spp.
lily-of-the-valley	*Convallaria majalis*	willow	*Salix* spp.

The Language of Flowers

Since earliest times plants and flowers have been ascribed meanings, and these can be reflected in bridal bouquets. The traditional meanings of the flowers used in the bouquets included in this book are listed below, together with those of some other well-loved flowers.

alstroemeria: fortune, prosperity, wealth

amaranthus: immortality, unfading love

anemone: expectation, forsaken, death, fading youth, suffering

antirrhinum (snapdragon): strength, deception, gracious lady

asphodel (*Asphodelus*): my regret follows you to the grave

bay (*Laurus nobilis*): I change but in death

beech (*Fagus* spp.): prosperity

birch (*Betula* spp.): elegance, grace, meekness

bluebell (*Hyacinthoides non-scriptus*): constancy

bouvardia: enthusiasm

box (*Buxus* spp.): constancy, constancy in friendship, stoicism

calla lily (*Zantedeschia* spp.): beauty

camellia: admiration, perfection, gratitude, transience of life, good-luck gift (for a man); pink camellia: longing for you; red camellia: you're a flame in my heart; white camellia: adoration, perfection, loveliness, you're adorable

carnation (*Dianthus caryophyllus*): devoted love, fascination, bravery, friendship, vanity, pride, socialism; pink carnation: I'll never forget you, woman's love; red carnation: admiration, my heart aches for you; white carnation: innocence, pure love, sweet and lovely, good-luck gift (for a woman), you're adorable

chrysanthemum: contemplation, the onset of autumn; red chrysanthemum: I love you; white or green chrysanthemum: truth; yellow chrysanthemum: slighted love

clematis: ingenuity, artifice

cornflower (*Centaurea cyanus*): delicacy, refinement

crocus: cheerfulness, youthful gladness, resurrection and heavenly bliss

cyclamen: modesty, shyness, resignation, goodbye

dahlia: dignity, elegance, forever thine, good taste, instability

daisy (*Bellis perennis*): contempt for worldly goods, innocence

daylily (*Hemerocallis*): coquetry, Chinese emblem for mother

delphinium: ardent attachment, flight of fancy

eucharis: maidenly charm

euphorbia: persistence

fern: sincerity, fascination, magic, confidence, shelter; asparagus fern: fascination; maidenhair fern: secret bond of love, discretion; royal fern: reverie

fir: time

forget-me-not (*Myosotis* spp.): true love, remembrance, humility, longing for loyalty

forsythia: anticipation

foxglove (*Digitalis* spp.): youth, stateliness, insincerity

freesia: friendship, innocence, trust

fritillary (*Fritillaria* spp.): arrogance, pride

galax: encouragement

gerbera: innocence

gladiolus: generosity, sincerity, strength of character, natural grace

gloriosa: glorious beauty

grass: submission

gypsophila (baby's breath): innocence, purity of heart

heather (*Erica* spp.): protection, your wishes will come true

hippeastrum: expectation, splendid beauty, pride, timidity

honeysuckle (*Lonicera caprifolium*): lasting pleasure, permanence, steadfastness; woodbine (*L. periclymenum*): generous and devoted affection

hyacinth (*Hyacinthus orientalis*): playful joy, loveliness, death and revival; blue hyacinth: constancy; purple hyacinth: sorrow; white hyacinth: unobtrusive loveliness, I will pray for you; yellow hyacinth: jealousy

hydrangea: thank you for understanding, boastfulness, frigidity, heartlessness

iris: faith, hope, wisdom, authority, victory, conquest, pain

ivy (*Hedera* spp.): fidelity, wedded love, friendship, affection

jasmine (*Jasminum* spp.): amiability

lavender (*Lavandula* spp.): love, devotion

lilac (*Syringa* spp.): first emotion of love; white lilac: youthful innocence, modesty, virginity, majesty, purity

lily (*Lilium* spp.): lily (general) purity of heart; white lily: purity, virginity, majesty, it's heavenly to be with you; yellow lily: gratitude, happiness, I'm walking on air, false; Madonna lily (*L. candidum*): purity; Easter lily (*L. longiflorum*): purity, modesty

lily-of-the-valley (*Convallaria majalis*): return of happiness, sweetness, humility, you've made my life complete, fortune in love

lotus (*Nelumbo* spp.): enlightenment

mint (*Mentha* spp.): virtue

mistletoe (*Viscum album*): the state beyond earthly limitations

moluccella (bells of Ireland): good luck, truth

narcissus (daffodil): regard, you're the only one, unrequited love, unequalled love, egotism, formality, the sun shines when I'm with you; N. *pseudonarcissus* and *N. poeticus*: resurrection and rebirth
nasturtium (*Tropaeolum* spp.): patriotism

oak (*Quercus* spp.): leaves: bravery; acorn: symbol of life and immortality
orchid: beauty, love, refinement, beautiful lady, flower of magnificence

palm: success, victory, fame, righteousness
passionflower (*Passiflora caerulea*): the suffering of Christ
peony (*Paeonia* spp.): happy marriage, compassion, bashfulness, shame
phlox: unity, our souls are united
pine: hope, pity
pomegranate (*Punicum granatum*): compassion, fertility, immortality, intellectual ability, creative power
poppy (*Papaver* spp.): life and death, good and evil, light and darkness, fruitfulness
pussy willow: motherhood

ranunculus: charm, radiance
rose (*Rosa* spp.): happiness; deep pink rose: thankfulness; peach rose: desire and enthusiasm; orange rose: desire, enthusiasm, fascination; pale pink rose: grace, joy; pink rose: perfect happiness, secret love, grace and sweetness, indecision; red rose: secrecy; white or cream rose: innocence, purity; yellow or green rose: friendship, joy, jealousy
rosemary (*Rosmarinus* spp.): remembrance
rudbeckia: justice

snowdrop (*Galanthus nivalis*): hope
stephanotis: happiness in marriage, desire to travel, come to me
strawberry (*Fragaria vesca*): purity, sensuality, fertility, abundance
sunflower (*Helianthus annuus*): devotion, loyalty, pride
sweet pea (*Lathyrus odoratus*): blissful pleasure, delicate pleasure, goodbye, departure, thank you for a lovely time

tulip (*Tulipa* spp.): love, passion, fame, perfect lover; red tulip: believe me, declaration of love; variegated tulip: beautiful eyes; yellow tulip: hopeless love, there is sunshine in your smile; *T. gesneriana*: wealth, importance, object of speculation

veronica (speedwell): fidelity

water lily (*Nymphaea* spp.): purity of heart

Index

Acknowledgements

All photography except pages 6, 9 and 13 has been supplied courtesy of IPC Images/ IPC Media Limited 020 72617077

Photolibrary.com/**Banana Stock** 6 /**Stockbyte** 9 /**Digital Vision** 13

IPC Images/ IPC Media Limited/ **Sue O'Brien** 2, 4, 14, 16, 17, 18, 19, 20, 21, 22, 23, 24, 25, 26, 27, 28, 29, 30, 31, 32, 33, 34, 35, 36, 39, 40, 43, 44, 45, 46, 47, 48, 50, 51, 52, 53, 54, 55, 56, 57, 58, 59, 60, 61, 62, 63, 64, 65, 66, 67, 68, 69, 70, 71, 72, 73, 75, 76, 78, 79, 82, 83, 84, 86, 87, 88, 89, 90, 91, 92, 93, 94, 96, 97, 99, 101, 102, 103, 105, 106, 107, 108, 109, 110, 112, 113, 114, 116, 118, 119, 120, 121, 123, 124, 126, 127, 128, 129, 131, 133, 134, 135, 136, 137, 138, 139, 141, 142, 143, 144, 145, 146, 147, 148, 150, 151, 152, 153, 154, 155, 156, 157, 158, 159, 160, 162, 163, 164, 165, 166, 167, 169, 170, 171, 172, 173, 174, 175, 177, 180, 181, 182, 183, 184, 185, 187, 188, 189, 190, 191, 192, 193, 194, 195, 196, 197, 198, 199, 200, 201, 202, 203, 205, 206, 207, 208, 209, 210, 212, 213, 214, 216, 217, 218, 219, 220, 221, 222, 223, 224, 225, 226, 228, 229, 230, 231, 233, 235, 236, 237, 238, 239, 240, 242, 243, 244, 245, 246, 247, 248, 249, 251, 252, 253, 254, 255, 256, 257, 259, 260, 263, 264, 266, 267, 268, 269, 270, 273, 275, 276, 278, 280, 282, 283, 284, 287, 288, 289, 290, 292, 295, 296, 298, 299, 300, 301, 304, 305, 307, 308, 309, 310, 311, 312, 314, 315, 316, 317, 318, 319, 320, 321, 322, 323, 324, 325, 327.

/ **Roy Sams** 1, 37, 38, 41, 42, 49, 74, 77, 80, 81, 85, 98, 100, 104, 111, 115, 117, 122, 130, 132, 140,161, 168,176, 178, 186, 204, 211, 215, 227, 232, 234, 241, 250, 258, 261, 262, 271, 272, 274, 277, 279, 281, 285, 286, 291, 293, 294, 302, 303, 306, 313, 326.

Thanks to Andrea Ventress, Deputy Editor of *Wedding* and *Wedding flowers* and her team for all their help in compiling and editing this book.

Wedding[TM] and *Wedding flowers*[TM] are both Trade Marks of IPC Media, © IPC Media Limited 2006. *Wedding flowers* is a brand extension of *Wedding* magazine.

Executive Editor Katy Denny
Project Editor Leanne Bryan
Editor Lydia Darbyshire
Design Manager Tokiko Morishima
Design Janis Utton
Senior Production Controller Manjit Sihra
Picture Research Assistant Aruna Mathur

To subscribe to *Wedding* magazine call 0845 6767778 OR click on www.ipcmedia.com